The
Inflations & Deflations
of the Spencer Family

By Nick Peacey

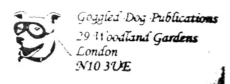

Goggled Dog Publications
29 Woodland Gardens
London
N10 3UE

Acknowledgements

———— • — • — • ————

Writing acknowledgements for a book that has taken years to complete makes you realise just how much help you have received. Inevitably I will leave people out and to them I apologise in advance.

I am particularly grateful to:
- Graham, Dorothy and Charles Spencer and Amanda Mehigan (nee Spencer) for their information, resources and backing for a book about the family. (Their images are credited as 'Courtesy the Spencer family')
- Alan Harvey for all his genealogical research and contacts
- Ruth Fryer for her ideas, images and discussions about the family
- Nick Clayton and John Green of the Veteran-Cycling Club for checking the cycling history
- Robert Pankhurst for checking the section on geology
- Hilary Deeble-Rogers and Justin Bickersteth of Highgate Cemetery Trust
- John Baker of the British Balloon Museum and Library and Andrew Renwick of the Royal Air Force Museum
- Colin Houghton for his thoughtful comments on drafts
- Cate Rae of Widgit for the website design
- Rachel Fletcher and the team at RF Design, particularly Gemma Tovee who has made it look so good
- Gill Willoughby, my sister, and her husband David, for all the support over the years
- Lindy, Sarah and Caroline Peacey for the improvement of drafts, tolerance of the writing time and fantastic encouragement of the whole project

The book would not have been possible without the work of these family record keepers whose contributions are not fully recognised in the text:
- Ena (Victorine), the only child of Auguste Gaudron and Marina (nee Spencer), whose reminiscences of family life appear throughout the book
- Marie Townend (nee Spencer), the eldest daughter of Percival and Mary Spencer, who pulled together many strands of the family history during the 1940s and 50s
- Dorothy Spencer-Clarke (nee Spencer), the second daughter of Percival and Mary Spencer, who kept many records which have now passed to the British Balloon Museum and Library

Contents

fig. 1. Robert Cocking and his parachute

Robert Cocking's Experiment

At eight o'clock on the warm evening of the 24th July 1837 Robert Cocking decided to leave his companions. He called to them, 'Good night, Spencer, good night, Green'.

At the Greenwich Observatory in south-east London, Professor George Airey, the Astronomer Royal, watched the leave-taking through a telescope. Robert Cocking was over a mile above him in a small wicker basket hanging from something that looked like a giant upside down lampshade. Three strong ropes attached this contraption to the basket of a balloon, the *Great Nassau*, fifty feet above. In that basket were Charles Green, aeronaut, and Edward Spencer, solicitor and part-time aeronaut.

For Robert Cocking was about to launch himself into space on a parachute of his own design. He had barely tested this device and was the first person to make a parachute jump in England for thirty five years. But at 61 years of age he was, at long last, the star of a drama he had planned for most of his life.

Cocking was obsessed with balloons and parachutes. Charles Dickens' friend Henry Morley wrote that 'he drew balloons because he loved them, and delicately stroked with the sepia over their fat sides, as a lover strokes the curls of his mistress.'

The obsession with parachutes had its origins in September 1802. As a young man of 24 Cocking watched the Frenchman, Andre Jacques Garnerin, make a parachute descent from a balloon in London. Garnerin landed near St Pancras Church, just up the road from where the railway station would be built later in the century.

The penny ballad sellers recorded his exploit:

> *Bold Garnerin went up*
> *Which increased his repute*
> *And came safe to earth*
> *In his grand parachute.*

fig. 2. Edward Spencer, probably in 1837

We may wonder whether anyone ever paid as much as a penny for a ballad like that. In any case, the descent was not as easy as the rhyme suggested. Though Garnerin landed safely, his parachute oscillated fiercely and he was swung from side to side under the canopy. Some spectators claimed that Garnerin swung up so far that he was sometimes parallel to the ground and he and his parachute appeared to be travelling down side by side. Then and there Robert Cocking set his heart on making a parachute that would not treat its user like the pendulum of a grandfather clock.

In 1837 few people could see any point in parachutes at all. Even Charles Green, the most skilled balloonist of the day, said that he had an 'unconquerable objection' to the parachute which was 'a perfectly useless affair and unlikely to lead to any good end'. No Englishman made a parachute jump between Garnerin's displays in 1802 and Cocking's experiment in 1837.

Cocking believed that a parachute shaped like an upside-down lampshade would avoid the oscillation that had plagued Garnerin's efforts. He experimented with very small inverted cone parachutes and was pleased with the results. His lecture on his proposals at the London Institution in 1814 was such a hit that he was immediately asked to repeat it at the London Society of Arts.

fig. 3. Two types of parachute according to 'ES'

But there was a problem. No balloon had the lift to take Cocking's parachute anywhere near the height at which it could be tested until Charles Green designed and built the *Great Nassau*. It took up 20 men when tested at Vauxhall on the 21st September 1836. As soon he knew how powerful the balloon was, Cocking wanted to use it.

He probably persuaded Edward Spencer, a solicitor who acted as Green's 'co-pilot', that there was something in his views. An 'ES' contributed an informed article to a little periodical called *The Casket of Literature* on the 1st July 1837. The piece argues that an inverted cone parachute could avoid oscillation when falling like 'a common shuttle cock'. E.S says that the idea came from the 'scientific men of France' some 40 years earlier. Like Green, he takes a dim view of the parachute's usefulness: 'Parachutes cannot be of the least utility and they require a balloon of extraordinary power to lift to any great altitude, which is the chief reason why they have been discontinued.'

Cocking was not discouraged. He entered negotiations with Gye and Hughes, the *Nassau's* owners, who also owned Vauxhall Pleasure Gardens by the river Thames, and persuaded them that Charles Green should help test his ideas. Green, Cocking and Edward Spencer, making their first flight, ascended from Surrey Zoological Gardens on the 23rd May 1836. The aeronauts took up a cage containing a monkey called Jacopo. At an appropriate height, Cocking attached the cage to a small 'inverted cone' parachute and threw Jacopo, cage and parachute out of the basket. The monkey made a perfect descent and landed softly. George Spencer, one of Edward's sons, suggested in 1909 that Jacopo's triumph encouraged Robert Cocking to risk his life a few months later.

But Cocking still had to persuade Gye and Hughes of the worth of the full-scale parachute

fig. 4. The Great Nassau balloon lifting Cocking and his parachute

experiment. While gate receipts were likely to be substantial, they were worried about damage to their reputations from what many saw as a suicidal experiment.

John Bacon, close friend of a later generation of Spencers, certainly believed that Gye and Hughes were worried about the trial. In *Dominion of the Air*, Bacon describes a last minute attempt to save Cocking from himself. 'The proprietors of the gardens, as the hour approached, did their best to dissuade the over-confident inventor, offering, themselves, to take the consequences of any public disappointment.'

The Gardens had hosted every sort of high and lowbrow entertainment, including many balloon ascents. But this was way out of the usual run. The possibility of death and disaster had drawn thousands to pay two shillings and sixpence a head, an expensive entry fee, and cram through the gates. Thousands more, who could not afford the entrance fee or had left it too late to get a ticket, filled the streets outside and perched on any wall, building or window ledge they could find.

The *Great Nassau* balloon towered at the centre of the gathering. The balloon's top was now as tall as the roof of a four-storey house: the scarlet and white striped envelope of sheer Italian silk was almost full.

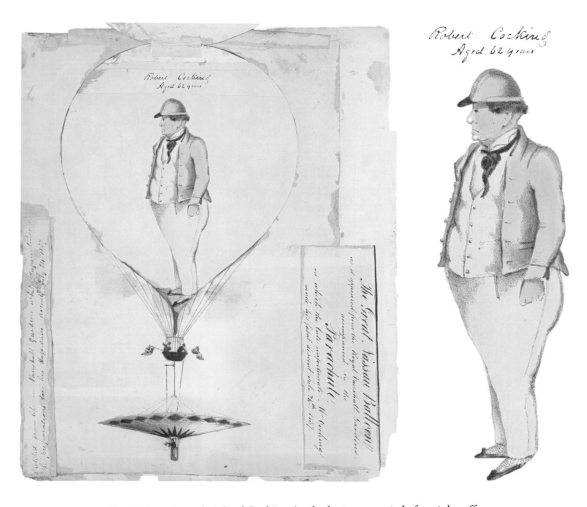

fig. 5. A unique sketch of Cocking in the last moments before take-off

But by six o'clock nothing much had happened and the crowds were getting restive. Delay was dangerous for aeronauts: a frustrated crowd easily became a mob. But the coal gas that had pumped into the *Great Nassau* all morning and afternoon had finally done its work and the balloon was pulling urgently against the ropes that held it to the ground. Charles Green climbed into the wicker basket under the envelope. Edward Spencer followed his friend into the basket and took his place beside him. At a command from Green, his assistants detached some weights and let out ropes to allow the balloon and the aeronauts to rise forty feet clear of the ground.

The assistants could then position the circular parachute, 34 feet across, under the balloon. They fastened it to ropes that dangled from the basket. Then, little by little, the *Great Nassau* was allowed to rise again. It drew the parachute slowly up from the ground and revealed it as an inverted, shallow cone covered in linen and decorated with brightly painted red and blue diamonds.

The assistants had one final task to perform: a small wicker balloon basket was attached to the bottom of the parachute. By 7.35 pm Robert Cocking's creation was ready to fly. He chatted to reporters as he waited for preparations to be complete. The *Greenwich, Woolwich and Deptford Gazette* and *West Kent Advertiser* observed him with care. 'Mr Cocking expressed by words the utmost confidence in the result of his experiment, but it appeared to us it was a confidence which he did not feel. His restless looks and nervousness of manner seemed to belie the bravery of his speech, and we thought more than once that he would willingly have postponed the attempt until a less hazardous trial had assured him of its safety.'

The Wonder magazine described the scene: 'The band of the Surrey Yeomanry played the National Anthem… a loud huzza proceeded from the ground and was re-echoed by the impatient mob outside. At this moment a tube or pipe of linen was lowered from the car of the balloon past the basket in which Mr Cocking was to sit…'

That tube needs explanation. To gain height, aeronauts normally emptied sandbags over the side of a balloon basket. But falling sand could damage the parachute's linen skin, so a cunning device, 'the tube or pipe of linen' was arranged to discharge sand below Cocking's basket.

The Wonder goes on, 'All preparations having been completed, Mr Cocking (having previously stripped off his coat as too cumbersome, and put on a light jacket) stepped into the car, amid the acclamations of the company. Some of his friends offered him a glass of wine which he drank…' Cocking shook all their hands.

Charles Green gave a final command to the ground crew 'Away'. All the ropes were released at the same moment. Amid deafening cheers, the triple-decker enterprise rose into the evening sky.

But ascent was slow. The combined weight of the parachute and Robert Cocking dragged down the *Great Nassau*, despite its lifting power.

The ballast-releasing device worked well for a moment or two and Spencer managed to send sixty pounds of sand down the discharge tube. But, as they were over Jacopo's home, Surrey Zoological Gardens, the parachute began to swing violently below the balloon and tore the tube out of place.

Green and Spencer now needed to hurl bags of ballast out beyond the parachute's rim to avoid damage to Cocking's creation. But throwing sandbags out before they were clear of the city could have killed someone on the ground. To fill the time, they began to divide the ballast into little packages for ease of throwing.

The laboured ascent continued. A light breeze carried the aeronauts east along the line of the Thames. Henry Coxwell saw the project moving down river and was unimpressed:

'…I saw it suspended in the air from London Bridge as it bore down Eltham way, and was struck with its cumbrous and rigid convex form, so ill adapted, I thought, to offer sufficient resistance, and to possess adequate strength for reaching the ground in safety.'

The aeronauts left the city and, in the light of the setting sun, began to travel over farmland. Green and Spencer could time their throws of the bags of ballast to the rhythm of the parachute's swings. They quickly threw out 50 pounds, and then, little by little, another 400. The balloon gained height slowly and climbed through thin cloud to 5,000 feet.

Cocking had wanted to start his parachute descent from 7,000 feet. But the *Great Nassau*, for all its 70,000 cubic feet of gas, could haul the experimenter and his creation no higher. Charles Green warned Cocking the limit had been reached.

Cocking decided to make his descent immediately and asked where they were. Spencer told him they were on a level with Greenwich. Green, who was never enthusiastic about the project, gave Cocking one last chance to call off his experiment. But Cocking was determined. Green asked him if he felt quite comfortable and if the practical trial had borne out his calculations. Green's own words explain what followed. 'Mr Cocking replied, "Yes,

I never felt more comfortable or more delighted in my life", presently adding, "Well, now I think I shall leave you." I answered, "I wish you a very good night and a safe descent if you are determined to make it and not use the tackle." The tackle was a device to allow Cocking to abandon the experiment and climb up into the balloon. Mr Cocking's only reply was, "Goodnight Spencer, goodnight, Green!"'

They were Cocking's last words. He pulled hard on the thin trigger rope that operated a catch to release the parachute from the balloon. Nothing happened. So he wrapped the rope round his wrist to get a better purchase and tugged again. This time he managed to free the parachute from the balloon. The action nearly killed all three of them. The *Great Nassau*, lightened of the terrific load, rocketed upwards.

Green wrote: 'The immense machine which suspended us between 'heaven and earth', while it appeared to be forced upwards with terrific velocity and rapidity through unknown and untravelled regions amidst the howlings of a fearful hurricane, rolled about as though revelling in a freedom for which it had long struggled, but of which until that moment it had been in utter ignorance. It, at length, as if somewhere fatigued by its exertions, gradually assumed the motions of a snake working its way with extraordinary speed towards a given object. During this frightful operation the gas was rushing in torrents from the upper and lower valve [of the balloon], but more particularly from the latter, as if the density of the atmosphere through which we were forcing our progress pressed so heavily on the valve at the top of the balloon as to admit of but a comparatively small escape by this aperture.'

The aeronauts would have collapsed from lack of oxygen, but Green had prepared a large silk bag which had been inflated by bellows with fifty gallons of air before they took off. 'The moment we felt ourselves going up… Mr Spencer, as well as myself, placed either of them [breathing tubes from the airbag] in our mouths. By this simple contrivance we preserved ourselves from instant suffocation. The gas, notwithstanding all our precautions, from the violence of its operations on the human frame, almost immediately deprived us of sight, and we were both, as far as our visionary powers were concerned, in a state of total darkness for four or five minutes.'

Meanwhile, far below them, the parachute and its inventor were hurtling to the ground. The design of the parachute was part of the problem, but human error may have made disaster inevitable. Cocking had been warned against holding onto the rope that freed the parachute from the balloon once the release had worked: it was attached to the balloon and would pull him up with it. But he forgot this vital instruction and wound the release cord round his arm. Frederick Gye told the inquest that he and Edward Spencer had found a deep cut around Cocking's left wrist when the body was examined.

As the *Great Nassau* shot up like a rocket, the line round Cocking's wrist would have jerked him out of his basket and slammed him against the parachute's lower hoop, which was made of tin tube. Henry Coxwell suggests that a wound found on Cocking's temple could well have been caused by this 'concussion'. Then, almost instantly, the thin cord would have broken and he would have been hurled back into the basket again.

The wreck of the parachute followed swiftly. Professor Airey, the Astronomer Royal, reported that the collapse of the parachute's shape only took three or four seconds. Airey suggested at the inquest that the hoops of thin metal tubing that had been used as the framework of the parachute caused the collapse. But Frederick Gye demonstrated by hanging weights from sections of the tubing that it should have been up to the task. He felt that the damage was done when Cocking's body crashed into the lower framework of the parachute. Charles Green and Michael Faraday, no less, supported this view.

Whatever the causes, far from descending without oscillation, the released parachute

The Ascent of the Royal Nassau Balloon from Vauxhall, with the Parachute attached.

The fatal Descent of the Parachute by which Mr Cocking lost his life.

fig. 6. The collapse of the parachute

swung crazily from side to side. The basket eventually broke away from its 'canopy' and fell, with Cocking still in it, separately for the last few hundred feet. It smashed into the ground at Lee Green, near the Dover Road to the south east of London. Cocking was alive when he was found but was unable to speak. He died as he was being taken for medical attention.

Far above, Green and Spencer only just survived. Their sight eventually came back. They had gone up to at least 24,000 feet, or four and a quarter miles high, and may well have set a world altitude record. At that moment, they are unlikely to have cared. Finally the balloon began to descend.

But there was so little gas that the floppy envelope could not slow the descent to a manageable speed. The aeronauts had to throw everything moveable out of the basket to give Green just enough lift to land the balloon relatively gently near Town Malling in Kent at 8.45pm. Edward Spencer, who recorded the location of each of his landings on the back of a visiting card as soon as the first local ran up and confirmed it, wrote his note in a shaky scrawl that night.

They did not learn the fate of Robert Cocking until the following morning. In fact, by the time Green landed the *Nassau*, farm labourers had carried the body, on a piece of fencing, across the fields of Lee Green Farm for a few hundred yards and then across the London Road (now the A20) into the Tigers Head public house. The corpse was laid out on a table downstairs. The remnants of the parachute were brought in and put in an upstairs room.

But indignity did not end for poor Cocking with his plunge from the sky. Early next morning the landlord put doorkeepers outside the rooms and charged sixpence to see the body and another sixpence to see the parachute. The head gardener of Vauxhall Gardens, who was keeping an eye on the Gardens' interests, saw the sacrilege and galloped off to find his bosses for support in putting a stop to it.

According to the inquest report, the landlord had taken £20, equivalent to 800 sixpences and at least 400 visitors, before two young members of the Gye family rode up and 'remonstrated' with him. Their fury stopped the exhibition of Cocking's body. But it was only when the local constable finally turned up that the parachute show came to an end.

The local coroner, Mr Carrtar, arrived close behind the constable and arranged an inquest. It took place in the Tigers Head and lasted two days. Presumably the landlord again profited from the proceedings.

When the inquest opened, Henry Cocking, the experimenter's grandson, identified the body. Then John Chamberlain, a shepherd, who had been first on the scene, testified about Cocking's fall... The balloon 'came down like thunder, that is in respect of the noise...it frightened the sheep.' As Chamberlain rushed where Cocking fell, he heard one groan, but nothing afterwards. 'The deceased was in the basket ...he did not move his eyes nor any part of his body. His wig was at a short distance from his head.'

Cocking's injuries were horrific. Charles Green made a statement. 'Mr Cocking was not thrown out of the basket but received a terrible wound on the right temple, and had his ancle dislocated... He was immediately attended by Dr Chowne who was on the spot...The unfortunate gentleman was not quite dead but in a few moments he ceased to exist. '

Chamberlain's master, a landowner called Mr Norman, said that he had arrived shortly afterwards with his servant, Thomas Grisdall. He had sent the shepherd off to fetch some hurdles while Grisdall pulled Cocking out of the basket.

A surgeon, identified as F.C.Finch, had seen the fall: he described the parachute as assuming the shape of an 'oyster shell diving through the water.' Contemporary illustrations show the parachute in this configuration. Finch had reached the scene quickly and had tried, as a bizarre form of first aid, to bleed Cocking.

Mr Gye from Vauxhall Gardens explained that he had made several suggestions about strengthening the parachute but 'the deceased declined to adopt them on account of the additional weight.'

The affair excited enormous interest. Twenty thousand people visited the spot where Cocking fell. Many, according to one paper, showed great interest in a patch of dried blood on the ground. This was not Cocking's blood. One of the first people on the scene, a young man, had taken one look at the awful sight and fainted. A medical man of some sort – could it have been F.C. Finch again?- had come forward and bled him.

There is nothing inherently unstable about an inverted cone shaped parachute. A few days after Cocking's death, an aeronaut called Mrs Graham demonstrated a small Cocking-style parachute at Cheltenham. She took up with her a chimpanzee called Mademoiselle Jennie. Mademoiselle Jennie, like the pioneer Jacopo, made a successful descent. Later on, John Wise, a famous American aeronaut, tested both Garnerin's and Cocking's designs and concluded that Cocking's could have worked well.

Cocking was buried in the churchyard of St Margaret's, Lee, not far from where he fell. Charles Green arranged and piloted a benefit flight for his widow within a fortnight; the fund that was opened raised more money still. Queen Victoria, who had been on the throne for 35 days, sent £50.

Charles Green went on to far more successful feats of aeronautics. By 1840 he had enough money to buy the *Great Nassau* for himself and was for many years a highly respected professional aeronaut. Edward Spencer flew with his friend frequently. His family became the most famous British aeronauts of the nineteenth and early twentieth century.

fig. 7. Edward Spencer used visiting cards to note where his flights landed

II

Edward Spencer senior

Edward Spencer had lived in London for all his 38 years when Cocking's experiment made him a national celebrity.

The Spencers had Welsh origins. About 1765, Edward's grandparents, John and Sarah Spencer, moved from Llanrwst in Montgomery, north Wales to Whitechapel, east London. About the same time, other Welsh 'immigrants', John and Sarah Tannatt, settled in nearby Shoreditch. The families may have known one another, as John Tannatt's mother had also lived in Llanrwst.

In August 1787, Edward Spencer, John and Sarah's eldest son, married Mary, the Tannatts' younger daughter, in St Leonard's Church, Shoreditch. Their son, Edward, was born in 1799.

His parents sent Edward Spencer to a little 'dame' school in Pentonville near his home. The first surviving result of his education is a huge black ink splodge on an handwriting exercise dated Christmas 1807. A second try with the same date, this time on a Harvest Home 'poster', is neater.

In 1810 he went on to St Pauls School, then trained at Lincoln's Inn as a solicitor and eventually settled on a career representing debtors in the insolvency courts.

He put his handwriting practice to good use in an intricately calligraphed Valentine to someone he called 'the adorable Diana'. The recipient was a young woman called Diana Snoxell. The Valentine seems to have done the trick: Edward and Diana were married at St Michael's Church, Cornhill, on the 11th May 1822.

Diana Snoxell came from another middle class London family. Her father, William Snoxell, was churchwarden at St Bride's Church, Fleet Street. The Snoxells were always better off than the Spencers. William ran a family business which had made window blinds since at least 1811. His son, William, took over the firm at his father's retirement, sold 'white spring roller blinds' to Charles Dickens for his smart new house in Devonshire Terrace in November 1839, and patented the roller blind in 1845.

To the adorable Dianna.

Virtue, reason, love and truth,
Are the richest joys of youth;
Let these ever be your care,
Endless joys you then will share;
Never from the truth depart,
This will give a peaceful heart.
In virtue you may find a charm,
Nought can woe so much disarm.
E'er let reason guide your choice
Salutary is her voice.
Dearest maid to love incline
And yourself to me resign
I swear I love you Valentine.

I remain

Your most devoted everlasting slave

VALENTINE.

fig. 8. Edward's Valentine card to 'the adorable Diana'

The families were linked twice again: James and John Snoxell, Diana's brothers, married Edward's younger sisters, Harriet and Anne. They should all have lived sensible lives in civilised places between Highbury and the City of London.

They did not. Eccentricity and invention were richly distributed through both the Snoxell and Spencer family trees. George Spencer described his uncle William: 'He was a clever man, but, like many other clever people, eccentric. His eccentricity was a mania for clocks and mechanical figures.'

Diana Snoxell brought resilience and a sense of humour to the marriage. Her granddaughter remembered how she enjoyed startling passersby who stared too long at the family's parrot in the window by thumbing her nose at them. As we learn of her life with Edward Spencer we may feel she needed all that resilience.

We have pen portraits of Edward Spencer. James Burden was Deputy Governor of Whitecross Debtors Prison, where Edward worked. Burden wrote a ponderous, but not entirely unfair, sketch for the Spencer family album.

A Character
Il Penseroso Spenceroso

He is as honest a fellow, as his profession [as a lawyer] will permit.

He is a good husband, I believe, (altho' I have received no advices from his wife on the subject), and is indisputably a tender Parent.

He has however one fault, too often there are times when he is "above" his clients, the Courts of Law, his wife, his Family and every other earthly consideration.

How inconsistent is man, an affectionate Husband and a tender Parent one hour, and the next, regardless of every Tie, urged either by pride or curiosity, disguised in the garb of Science, he takes an airy flight soaring above his Mother Earth and looking down with contempt on the plodding dwellers of mere Earth.

Thus puffed up and inflated, he rises above the sphere of his fellow man, sups with the Great Bear and sleeps with Venus, breakfasts in the Milky Way (not whey) and condescends to dine in Brunswick Parade, White Conduit Fields.'

Edward Spencer was less heroic at home than he was thousands of feet up in the air. Marie Townend, his great granddaughter, wrote on a family tree compiled just after the Second World War:

'Edward Spencer was so afraid of draughts that he always went to bed with his hat and muffler on and insisted on a candle alight on every stair to see him up & ...his wife,[Diana] used to follow him up blowing each one out. He also was so nervous about burglars that he often slept downstairs in the library: it is said that once a burglar did break in but was so scared at seeing someone in bed that he fled in panic.'

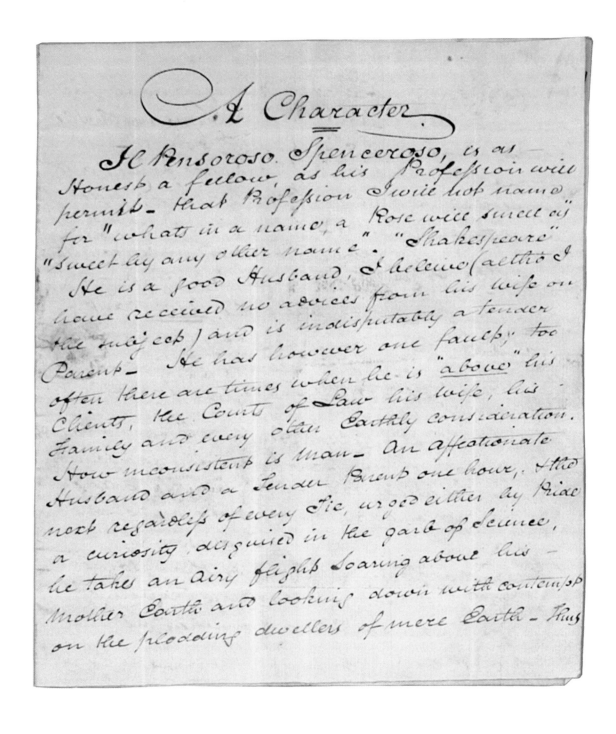

A Character

Il Pensoroso. Spenceroso, is as
Honest a fellow, as his Profession will
permit— that Profession I will not name
for "whats in a name, a Rose will smell as"
"sweet by any other name". "Shakespeare"
He is a good Husband, I believe (altho' I
have received no advices from his Wife on
the subject) and is indisputably a tender
Parent— He has however one fault; too
often there are times when he is "above" his
Clients, the Courts of Law his Wife, his
Family and every other Earthly consideration.
How inconsistent is Man— An affectionate
Husband and a Tender Parent one hour, the
next regardless of every Tie, urged either by Pride
a curiosity, disguised in the garb of Science,
he takes an airy flight soaring above his
Mother Earth and looking down with contempt
on the plodding dwellers of mere Earth— Thus

fig. 9. James Burden's pen portrait of Edward Spencer

20

But some things seem to have proceeded normally enough, despite the Spencers' idiosyncratic bedtime habits. Diana gave birth to three girls and four boys over a twenty year period. The first child, Edward, was born in 1823 and the youngest, Charles Green, named after his godfather the aeronaut, in 1837.

The younger Edward had a staid life for a Spencer. He was a competent draughtsman and water-colourist, who published a drawing of the Edinburgh Fire Balloon in the *Literary World* magazine in 1840 when he was 17. He became a clerk in the post office and pursued enthusiasms that included drawing, painting and singing bass with the Sacred Harmonic Society. He stuck mementoes of these concerts, including entry tickets for the opening of the 1851 Great Exhibition and a Buckingham Palace concert in 1864 into a large scrapbook. As the family archivist, he also preserved cuttings, drawings and accounts of his father's balloon adventures, along with notebooks and bits and pieces from family life.

So we know that from the 1820s Edward Spencer senior was fashionably consumed with scientific curiosity. He worked his way through a library of books that included *Pepys' Diary*, which had only been deciphered in 1826, *The Principles of Matter, Kendal's Pocket Encyclopaedia,* (all the way through from page one) the *Philosophy of Mineralogy, Paley's Evidences of Christianity, A Sketchbook* by Geoffrey Cryon, Gent., and acres and acres of William Cobbett.

Edward recorded the cost of canal-building in the United States (£3105 per mile) and England (£5060 per mile); the height of Strasbourg Cathedral ('549 feet: only surpassed by that of the Great Pyramid'); the causes of syphilis (which he camouflaged with its own shorthand designation, presumably to discourage interest by the wrong sort of reader: his wife? his children? Mary Ann the servant?); the Grub Street view of English journalists 'they seem to have a natural propensity to swallow incredible stories as Rooks have to swallow worms and grubs'); and, of course, natural history 'the herbivorous animals have not the power of vomiting'.

Edward wrote up his interests in the twopenny magazine *The Casket of Literature*. Heads on spikes above London Bridge in Elizabeth I's reign, Signor Campanari's exhibition of Etruscan artefacts and the latest gossip on aeronautics all went into the mix.

He liked curiosities and their collectors and was proud of his coin of the emperor Hadrian excavated near the new London Bridge. In December 1848, an evening with Charles Green and the coin collector William Till resulted in a slightly drunken 'Letter of Friendship', signed *CG aeronaut, ES aeronaut, and William Till, no aeronaut at all.*

Geology and what we today call palaeontology were dominant enthusiasms for a time. Edward became a Fellow of the Geological Society of London in 1829. In 1835 he read the Society a paper called 'Observations on the diluvium of the vicinity of Finchley, Middlesex. He wrote the paper out in one of his notebooks with this introduction, ' Presented by me to the Geological Society of London, at Somerset House, and read at their meeting of the January 1835 [in pencil] but not to my knowledge printed in their transactions-altho' I received their vote of thanks for my paper.'

Edward's paper describes what is now a well-known geological feature of north London. He had probably learned about this when the family lived in Wood Lane in Highgate. Gravel excavations had revealed a strip of unusual deposits about 150 yards wide and 15 to 20 feet thick running across the line of the Great North Road, now the A1, in East Finchley.

Edward's paper explains that the fragments in the deposit are, 'even of the most distant ages from the Granitic and Porphyric [porphyritic] rocks in Scotland to the Chalk inclusive' along with fossils, such as 'many perfect ammonites', more typical of other parts of England and, occasionally, 'detached vertebrae of gigantic Saurian reptiles… 4 inches in diameter some of which bear the appearance of attrition being imperfectly rounded.' …'on examining its general appearance the first opinion an observer is likely to form, is, that the operating cause which produced this phenomenon must have taken or have been removed far from the locality-probably some hundreds of miles'

This is sound enough, but then Edward wades into controversy. He writes, 'The subject of Diluvial Phenomena in England appears to the Author of this paper to deserve a greater degree of attention from geologists than has been generally bestowed to it.' The term 'diluvium' suggests that he saw a flood, probably the biblical Flood, as the force responsible for the movement of all this material.

The respect with which Edward quotes William Buckland reinforces this view. Buckland was a founder of the Society, with a 'passionate desire to reconcile geology and the Scriptures'.

Edward did not know, or did not accept, that the mass of water moving those fragments from all over England was frozen at the time. The deposit is the 'high tide mark' of a gigantic glacier that stopped just short of the site that is now East Finchley underground station. When the ice melted back to the north as the temperature rose, it left behind the chaotic jumble described by Spencer, just as an ebbing tide leaves a band of jetsam across the beach.

The 'diluvium' theory was under pressure by the time Edward gave his paper. In 1834 Searles V. Wood junior published an article in the Geological Society's journal on 'The Structure of the post Glacial deposits of the South-East of England.' The great and good of the Society may have felt that Edward's offering was a bit behind the times. The publications committee concluded that it was not of sufficient interest to justify publication in full, but that a note of 'one or two curious statements' was worth recording in their Transactions.

Jack Whitehead, an eloquent historian of north London, reprinted a paper on the deposit by a Dr Wetherell, a Highgate general practitioner who became a geologist. Edward does not mention him. Did he think he should be recognised as the discoverer or was he trying to beat Wetherell to publication?

If Edward Spencer's writing on geology fell into the mud of a changing paradigm, he had one achievement that no-one could take away. He was a fan of the French scientist Cuvier. Cuvier had fossil-hunted on the Isle of Sheppey so Edward went there too.

This was a good idea. On Sheppey Edward found the fossil head of a small prehistoric crocodile. After his discovery, other parts of similar creatures began to be recognised elsewhere in England. Edward had found a new species. This was named *crocodylus Spenceri*. Buckland (that man again) described it in 1837: ' True crocodiles with a short and broad snout like that of a Cayman or Alligator appear for the first time in strata of the tertiary period.'

You can see the crocodile's head at the Natural History Museum in London. Considering it is 40 million years old, the creature looks remarkably like any little crocodile living today. As the curator from the Natural History Museum put it when showing me the head: 'Nature's rule is: if it ain't broke, don't fix it.' Crocodile design has not needed fixing for a long, long time.

The Geological Society finally published a note on Edward's paper in 1838. The note does not mention the Flood or the diluvium. But by then Edward may well have lost interest. He was now a famous aeronaut and resigned from the Society in December 1838.

Edward Spencer spent some time on the ground being a lawyer. His son George described his father's journey to work from Highgate in the 1830s and 40s: 'My father was a solicitor and used often to have to walk to and from the City. That was when he happened to miss the mail coach-the only possible conveyance in those days. But it was a pleasant enough walk – fields and hedges all round and air you could breathe. I remember there was a hayfield where Jones Brothers, Holloway [Road – now a Waitrose], now stands.'

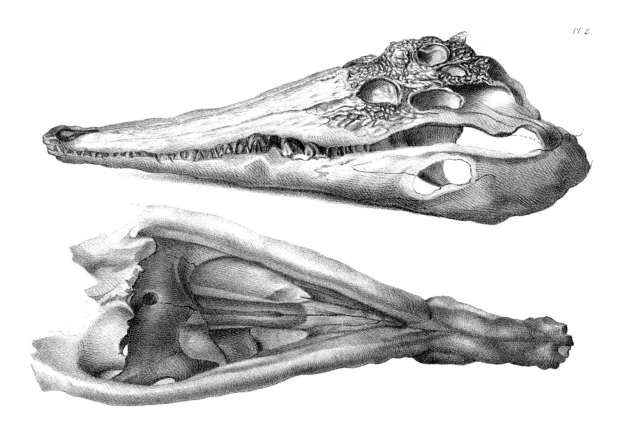

fig. 10. Edward Spencer's crocodile head found on the Isle of Sheppey

We have a description of Edward Spencer looking for work in the debtors' prison:

You see… however, about the gait of our attorney, a good deal of activity and energy; and his hands, like a pendulum, describing with equal activity and rapidity a considerable arch of a circle in a short time. He passes you, if not bent on some conversation in quest of clients, in the twinkling of an eye; but you would look for him as soon behind the counter of some bustling shop of St Pauls or Cheapside as at the desk of the red tape gentry.

…he smooths the way easily and gently to a friendly conversation, especially when things look auspicious. This man seldom solicits clients in person, performing, as he generally does, that part of the business by deputy.

There is little, about him or his person, which enables you to mark him out from the crowd. His dress! why, here you are at fault, for his black coat and coloured trousers, is the taste of his fashion. His face is rather full; his eyes smallish; with some remnant of brown whiskers running in the direction of his mouth… He is said to be related to Barrett the Keeper [of the Whitecross Street Prison], of which prospective clients are sometimes reminded, to which, however, we can have no objection.

Portraits do not suggest the whirling hands, coloured trousers or shopkeeperly aspect described in this sketch of Edward Spencer. They offer instead a well-shaven man of stylish professional gravitas, with blond (greatly thinned) hair and a clear gaze set off by a stock and the black coat.

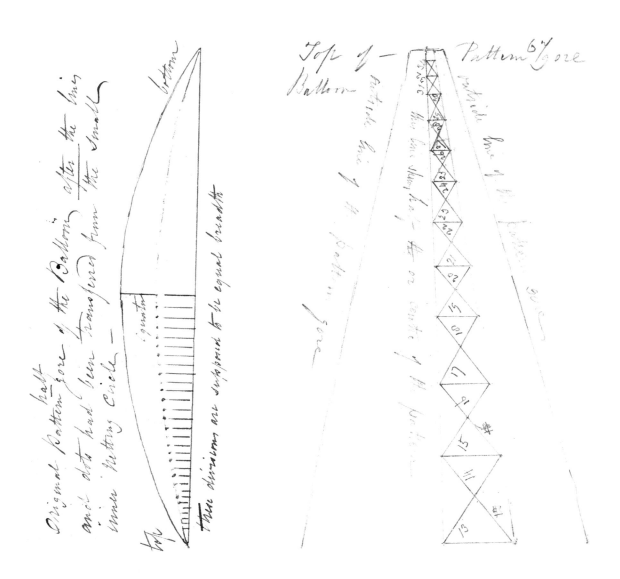

fig. 11. Designs for the 'gores' and netting of a balloon envelope from Edward's notebook.
Courtesy of the Spencer family

fig. 12. Fabric used in making the Great Nassau balloon

The portraits do not show his height: Edward's 1842 passport to le Havre gives him 1m 63 (5 feet 4 inches). Many of the Spencers have been short. Later photographs of the family as aeronauts often show them overshadowed by their passengers, let alone by the balloon.

Only one of Edward's court cases appears in the family album. It was one of the first heard under the 1843 Insolvent Debtors Act. This Act was part of the process of liberating debtors 'whose sufferings were really enough to make one's hair stand on end—any thing so abhorrent as the treatment of these unhappy people could not be imagined to exist in a civilized country' from the threat of gaol. The Act was designed to prevent the imprisonment of those who had become insolvent through negligence or incompetence, rather than fraud.

Edward lost the case: it was probably a long shot anyway. Commissioner of Bankruptcy Fonblanque, giving judgement, felt that Edward's client, a gold chain maker called Pearson, was not entitled to the protection of the Act, because his insolvency was incurred through 'breach of trust'. Pearson presumably went back to jail.

But Edward's real claim to fame was his collaboration with Green. After the Cocking disaster, he became Green's regular assistant pilot and recorder. The aeronaut and clergyman, JM Bacon, described the partnership: '[Green's] chosen friend and collaborator [was], Edward Spencer, of Barnsbury, who only nine years later [in 1845] compiles memoranda of thirty four ascents, made under every variety of circumstances, many being of a highly enterprising nature. We find him writing enthusiastically of the raptures he experienced when sailing over London in night hours, of lofty ascents and extremely low temperatures, of speeding twenty eight miles in twenty minutes, of grapnel ropes breaking, and of a cross-country race of four miles through woods and hedges. Such was Mr Spencer the elder and if further evidence were needed of his practical acquaintance with, as well as personal devotion to, his adopted profession of aeronautics, we have it in the store of working calculations and other minutiae of his craft, most carefully compiled in manuscript by his own hand; these memoranda being to this day consulted by his grandsons...'

One little notebook, crammed full of instructions and pencil sketches on building a superior 1840s balloon, has survived. You could have a good try at building a balloon with it today. Edward's son, Charles, and his sons certainly used it.

The detail is impressive. Here Edward describes sticking 'gores' of silk together to form the balloon's envelope. 'In cementing the seams of the balloon lay the composition [the 'glue', a mixture of copal and mastic varnish] with a pitch brush, rather than lay on two or three coats – not to put on a fresh coat until the other one feels very adhesive-a great deal depends on the weather sometimes an hour or two-sometimes 3 or 4 hours-sometimes all night.' And so it goes on, until your do-it-yourself balloon is complete and ready to ascend.

Bacon points out that for the Cocking experiment Green required an assistant 'of exceptional nerve and reliability'… He also notes the description of a flight by the writer and show business entrepreneur Albert Smith . 'On that occasion ten people went up, including Charles Green as skipper, and Edward Spencer, who, sitting in the rigging, was entrusted with the all-important management of the valve rope.'

Bacon was a Spencer fan, but even if we discard some of the ballast in his remarks, sufficient remains to suggest that Edward Spencer was a careful, brave and committed aeronaut. Charles Green certainly appreciated his help: he gave Edward a handsome barometer specially designed for aeronautical use. When flying over farmland someone dropped this barometer and it buried itself in the soil. Years later a ploughman recovered the barometer and it found its way back to the family who have it today (see page 123).

Unfortunately, none of Edward Spencer's notebooks describing his flights has made it down through the years, though some of the visiting cards on which he wrote details of each landing remain to tantalise us.

Charles Green's income was no more secure than that of any other aeronaut/showman. When business was poor in the 1820s, he sometimes attracted a crowd by ascending alone on a pony on a platform below the balloon. The Society for the Prevention of Cruelty to Animals was, unsurprisingly, outraged.

Edward Spencer's handwriting records a verse commentary on the event in *Aeronautica Illustrata*.

Lines on Charles Green the Aeronaut on the occasion of taking up his horse

E'en in this age of intellect
It does make people stare,
To see an Ass upon a horse
Ride up to take the Air.

Nor is his conduct to be blamed
But rather to be prais'd,
Who, while he strives to raise the wind,
E'en by the wind is raised.

Edward Spencer may not have written that poem. But he did produce an occasional Christmas cracker-style riddle about his friend:

Q.   Why is Charles Green the aeronaut like a spider?
A.   Because he is fond of taking a Fly.

The Spencer family moved from Highgate to Brunswick Parade (now part of Barnsbury Road) in Islington in the late 1830s. Sometimes they entertained the neighbours: 'an aerial Guy Faux' took place on the 5th November, 1839. 'At Mr Edward Spencer's, Guy Faux will make his first Aerial Ascent from the above House and Garden, at Four o'clock. After which, Mr Spencer will entertain his Friends with Tea, Coffee and cards; including certain savory creature comforts that constitute a substantial Supper. There will be a concert after supper. Mr Spencer will play the fiddle accompanied by two eminent musical professors on the Hurdy gurdy and Jews harp. Vivat Regina.'

Below we find: 'Second Edition, 5 o'clock pm. The above extraordinary event took place among the uproarious applause of gaping thousands. The inhabitants of Islington were absolutely spiflicated at this superhuman inflation of the immortal Guy.'

Green and Spencer were involved in one of the first scientific flights carried out in England. L.T.C Rolt says sadly, 'It is entirely typical of the England of that time that Green's undertaking was not sponsored by any scientific institution but was financed entirely by one private individual.'

The individual was George Rush, a rich Essex landowner, who wanted to trial a barometer he was developing. Green himself was keen to return to the altitudes he and Spencer had reached after releasing Cocking. Continental aeronauts were reporting improbable effects at high altitudes, including 'swelling heads' and bleeding from the eyes and ears on any ascent over 20,000 feet. Green and Spencer were determined to disprove this nonsense.

BALLOONING.

fig. 13. Punch's view of equestrian ballooning

Green, Rush and Spencer took off from Vauxhall Gardens on the 4th September, 1838. As Green put it in the account of his ascents written for Edward the younger's scrapbook on 16th April 1840. 'In 1838 I made 2 experimental flights with it [*the Great Nassau*]. The first took place on the fourth of September in company with Mr Rush and Mr Spencer and we attained an elevation of 19,335 feet, near 3 miles and three quarters.'

Charles Green described the celebration of their achievement in Rush's account of the flight. 'At our greatest elevation we charged our glasses, when Mr Rush gave the toast of our most gracious sovereign, Queen Victoria; the toast was drunk with great fervour and sincerity; we followed it by raising three cheers and "one cheer more" in honour of the deed; we lost no time in drinking the health of 'Her Royal Highness the Duchess of Kent, who gave birth to our gracious Queen.' Mr Rush then proposed the health of 'the two greatest commanders, his Grace the Duke of Wellington upon the earth, and Mr Green in the air,' this toast, like its predecessors, was responded to with alacrity, and accompanied with the usual honours.'

But the ascent was not high enough for the experiments Rush had in mind. So next time Green and Rush went up without Spencer and reached a height they claimed as 27,147 feet. They suffered nausea and cold. But their heads remained unswollen and their eyes and ears did not bleed.

Spencer flew with Charles Green, and sometimes with his son, Henry, right through the 1840s. He even maintained friendly relations with Henry Coxwell, Green's greatest rival

AERIAL GUY FAUX.

AT MR. EDWARD SPENCER'S,

11, BRUNSWICK PARADE,

Near the White Conduit Gardens, Islington.

This present, the 5th day of November, 1839, Guy Faux, will make his First
Ærial Ascent from the above House and Garden, at Four o'clock.
After which, Mr. SPENCER will entertain his Friends with Tea, Coffee, and
Cards ; including certain savory creature comforts that constitute a substantial
Supper.

THERE WILL BE A CONCERT AFTER SUPPER :

MR. SPENCER WILL PLAY THE FIDDLE,

Accompanied by Two Eminent Musical Professors

ON THE HURDY GURDY AND JEW'S HARP.

Vivat Regina.

(SECOND EDITION.)

FIVE O'CLOCK, P.M.

The above extraordinary Ascent took place amidst the uproarious applause
of gaping thousands. The Inhabitants of Islington were absolutely spifficated at
this super-human inflation of the immortal Guy. An express has just arrived,
per Cruelty Van, announcing its safe descent in those sylvan regions, Hare Street
Fields, Bethnal Green. It may be gratifying to Her Most Sacred Majesty, the
Royal Family the Nobility, Gentry, and Nobility of these realms, to learn that
Mr. SPENCER'S Concert came off with prodigious *eclat ;* the evening's enter-
tainments concluding with "Jim Crow," sung in character, by a Pious Missionary
from the Spanish Liquorice Islands, a Dance of Hop-Scotch, by a Converted
Nigger, and a Hornpipe by a Wooden Legged Professor of Terpsichore.

fig. 14. Aerial Guy Faux, November 1839

who wrote to him, probably in 1847, 'Come this evening and see Gale and myself ascend-a night ascent with fireworks. Don't fail as I long for a Chat with an old and valued friend.'

Edward Spencer did not live to grow old, reminisce about aeronautical exploits and see his children build on his 114 pioneering flights with Green. Despite all his adventures he died in his bed. We have a melancholy survival from his last few days, almost certainly his notes on a doctor's visit written on a scrap of paper from a child's writing practice book. They read like the last attempt of a man used to overcoming obstacles to keep a grip on what was happening to him. He had what was then called 'brain fever', perhaps a form of meningitis.

The smudged notes, beside which his son Edward wrote 'My Father's last letter', give a vivid picture of the 'prescriptions' for the dying man. They include 'Clothing-drawers and stockings-Mutton Broth, if absolutely necessary under existing circumstances-Am I to keep up a perspiration?-Is the head to be bathed or a wet rag applied constantly and during the night-with vinegar and water-Taken a fresh cold?- How often to wash the Mouth out with vinegar and water-Skin of lips peal [sic] off-What is my pulse?-Does this approach to typhus?-Brain fever-Not the least appetite but nevertheless to endeavour to eat a bit of bread and butter, oranges, toast and water which…'

Nothing Dr Burrows, the Spencers' doctor, could do made any difference. Edward Spencer died at home in Brunswick Parade on the 14th February 1849. He was not quite 50 years of age. His family buried him with ceremony in Highgate Cemetery. Daniel Butler, undertaker of Farringdon Street, invoiced Diana Spencer for nineteen pounds, eighteen shillings and one penny. The invoice records the use of 'The best pall…' and charges 18 shillings for the furnishing of '2 Mutes Equipt in Gowns, scarves, Staves, Covers, Hatbands and Gloves.' His son Edward later arranged for the erection of a handsome surround for the grave and a headstone showing a modestly understated balloon.

Diana was left under £100 in her husband's will; the funeral had cost her a fifth of that sum and she also had a doctor's bill for nine pounds to pay. On top of this, she had two children under 16 to support. She may well have felt that more work in the debtors' court and less time flying with Charles Green would have done the family fortunes no harm. By the time we meet up with her in the 1851 census she is almost certainly taking in lodgers at no 11. A couple called Mr and Mrs Arthur, one in HM Customs and the other a 'Professor of French' are staying in the house.

Edward could never have afforded to fly as a paying passenger in a balloon on any sort of regular basis. The young Henry Coxwell heard someone checking flight prices with Charles Green in the early 1830s: an ordinary flight cost £20 a passenger. Coxwell was depressed 'For my part I received a wet blanket to all my youthful aspirations. If that is the fee I thought, it will be many a day and hour before I can think of ascending.'

The will of Edward's mother-in-law, Diana Snoxell senior, who died in 1831, gives evidence of tension about her daughter's family finances several years before Edward took up aeronautics. The long document is mostly taken up with the establishment of a trust fund to secure the financial well-being of Diana, who was her only daughter.

The trustees of the fund were to pay any sum realised from sales of stock ' into the proper hands of her… Diana Spencer for her separate use exclusively [my emphasis] of her said Husband and without being subject to his debts [or] interference…'. The tough wording suggests that Edward's mother-in-law did not think much of him as a provider. This was all, of course, well before the passing of the Married Women's Property Act in 1882. An 1830s mother might well have worried about her daughter's financial future when her son-in-law put so much more energy into his 'aerostation' than his legal career.

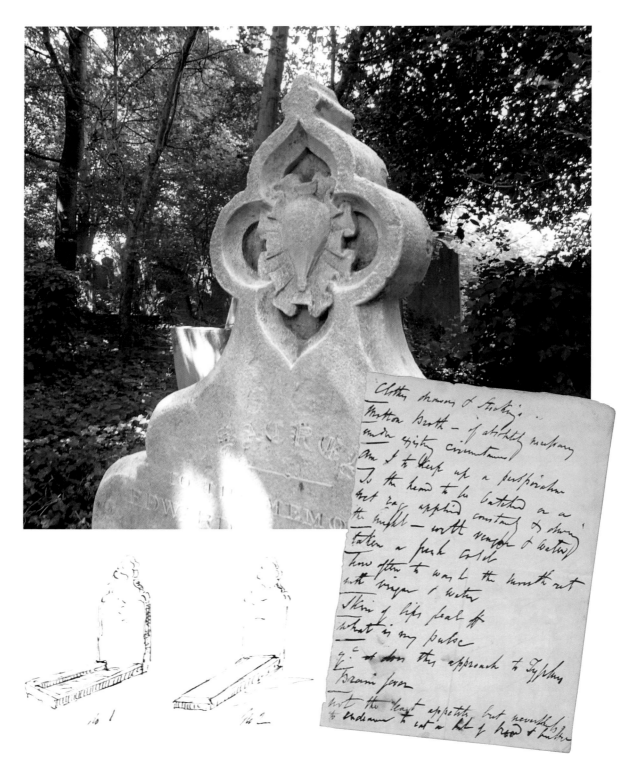

fig. 15–17. Edward Spencer's 'last letter' (right) with the family monument in Highgate Cemetery (top) and SJ Nicholl's choice of designs for the monument (left)

As James Burden put it,

'Man, man, thou are indeed an inconsistent Being-thou mournest the loss of a Descendant and yet when the Ascendant mood is on thee, thou takest thy aerial flight' deserting thy wife and all thy little ones. Methinks I hear Mrs. Spenceroso exclaim to thee:

> *'Thy flights, dear husband, know no bounds,*
> *So high you soar (and oft) gad zounds,*
> *Schedules, petitions all may go to crack*
> *And some day you may not come back.'*

We can only hope that the trust fund prospered.

fig. 18. Charles Spencer in St Petersburg

fig. 19. Entry ticket for a balloon ascent in Cremorne Gardens

• III •

Charles Green Spencer

The youngest son of Edward and Diana Spencer was born in 1837, the year his father found a fossil crocodile on Sheppey and shot to fame with the Cocking experiment. Charles Green Spencer's name proved appropriate. Of all Edward's children, he was to do most to build on his father's aeronautical legacy.

Charles joined his uncle William Snoxell's blind-making firm, probably as an apprentice at 14. George, his older brother, was already working there and would become managing director when Uncle William, who had no sons of his own, retired.

Charles may have first attracted notice through activities other than ballooning. In 1859, a Spencer, probably Charles, set out to walk a thousand miles in a thousand hours round and round Cremorne Gardens pleasure ground in Chelsea. Long distance walks, 'wobbles' or 'pedestrianism' were a popular method of fund-raising. At least two others had completed the task Charles had undertaken. A Captain Barclay covered 1000 miles in 1000 hours in July 1809 'for a wager on which thousands of pounds depended'. Richard Manks did the same thing at the Barrack Tavern Cricket Ground between the 17th June and the 29th July 1850 and won 'a considerable sum'

The Spencer album contains this cutting:

Cremorne Gardens

'The third juvenile festival attracted a large attendance to these delightful gardens on Thursday, but much disappointment was experienced with respect to out door amusements, owing to the unpropitious state of the weather… At eight o'clock last night Mr Spencer, who has engaged to walk 1000 miles in 1000 hours, completed the 419th mile; and although his looks bear symptoms of fatigue he feels confident of performing his task, which will not be concluded until the 3rd proximo.'

fig. 20. London, German Gymnasium in St.Pancras Road, 1866. Wood engraved print published in 'The Builder', 1866. Courtesy of ancestryimages.com

It seems unlikely Charles finished his walk or we would have heard a great deal more about it. We have no record of any time spent making roller blinds or even supervising their manufacture. We know, however, that he and George took up gymnastics in the 1850s. Charles travelled to Europe and quickly realised that German gymnastic equipment was far superior to that being made in England.

The brothers saw a business opportunity. Uncle William was persuaded to diversify and Snoxells expanded into the import, manufacture and sale of continental standard gymnastic apparatus. As an after sales service, the staff gave lessons to those who bought the equipment. This was not an obvious move for a window blind manufacturer, but was an inspired commercial decision. The firm made a steady income from the sale of equipment and gymnastics lessons; there was no competition in England for a long time.

Soon the firm was supplying the best-known professionals in the field, including Leotard, whose fame has now dwindled to the dimensions of an all-in-one PE costume.

John Mayall jr described the new approach to gymnastics in an article for *Ixion*, a magazine that Charles set up in 1875. Mayall was the son of the American-born photographer John Mayall, who took the first official photographs of Queen Victoria, Prince Albert and their family in the 1860s. Mayall explains how he and Charles Spencer were in at the beginning of 'real' gymnastics in England 'long before 1861'.

'Myself and a few friends… hired a sort of garden in Copenhagen Street, near Caledonian Road, and there Mr Spencer fitted up one of the earliest really efficient 'horizontal bars' that I know of in

England. To those like myself who commenced their gymnastic practice at the public gymnasium in Primrose Hill, the new 'horizontal–bar' with its steel core and thoroughly graspable thinness, was so great a luxury when compared with the clumsy, shaky and dangerous bars in the public Gymnasium that of itself it formed a most potent attraction…'

The gymnastic paradise became popular:

'we permitted first one or two professional gymnasts to visit us-then their friends came-and our garden became a favourite rendezvous for professionals and acrobats to such an extent that our little band of amateurs soon got outnumbered.'

So the amateur group moved their meetings to Charles Spencer's home where he had fixed up a horizontal bar and trapeze.

In 1861 many of the group joined the newly-established German Gymnastic Society. Snoxell's firm equipped the Society's gymnasium near Kings Cross in north London. This was a valuable contract. Mayall notes that at the time of writing the *Ixion* article the Society had expanded to 1500 members.

Charles Spencer described the scale of activity at the German Gymasium:

'I believe the majority of its members are English, but still the greatest credit is due to the Germans who originally established it… Here we see, in a noble central hall, spacious enough to allow three or four hundred to practise at one time, a large number of gymnasts going through the most varied exercises; some jumping over lines fixed between upright standards, the height being increased at each jump, others climbing knotted ropes hanging from roof girders about fifty feet in height; some engaged in vaulting on to or over the horses; two embryo athletes are seen enjoying a mild game at "see-saw", only that instead of sitting, they are hanging by their arms.'

And here let us observe that gymnastics is perhaps the least selfish occupation of the kind we can engage in, as there is "something for all" and we may see youths busily practising light exercises suitable to their powers, as well as stalwart men engaged in feats requiring the greatest amount of strength.'

Expertise was in short supply in the early days of the German Gymnasium.

'[Mayall] showed off with some exercises not commonly done by amateurs. I was much amused by being told by one of the persons in authority that such-like exercises were not approved by them; that they did not wish their members to join in such feats, and much more in the way of censure.'

But society members became more proficient:

'Members are themselves excellent judges of the kind of feats that are not too difficult or dangerous.'

Snoxells, which soon became Snoxell and Spencer, equipped other prestigious buildings, including the Crystal Palace in South London. As their reputation grew, they were commissioned to set up gymnasia in royal residences for Queen Victoria and the Prince of Wales, later Edward VII. It is hard to imagine either of those two soaring over a vaulting horse: the equipment was for the children.

This was a happy and prosperous time for Charles. Early in 1864 he had married Louisa Emma Woodward. Louisa came from a family that was eccentric even by Spencer standards.

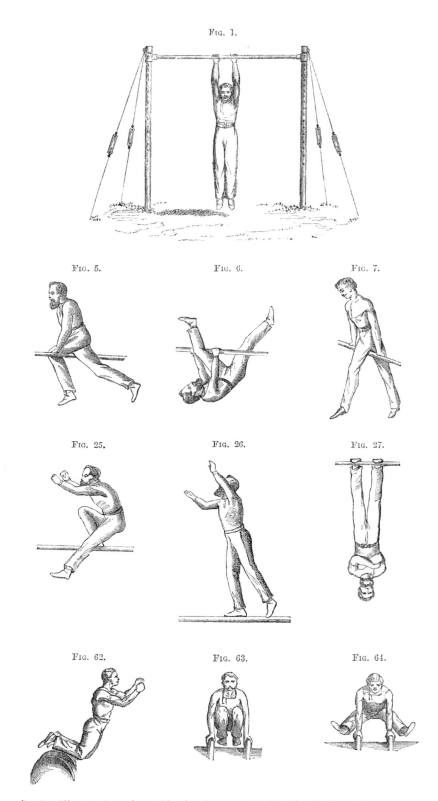

fig. 21. Illustrations from Charles Spencer (1866) The Modern Gymnast

Ena, Charles' grand-daughter, gives us the background:

'At an early age the legend goes she [Louisa's mother, another Marina] ran away with the 'son of a gentleman', that is he wasn't trained for and never did work. Grandma Woodward opened an eel pie shop in London. There were many children, possibly sixteen, of whom only five survived. It was said she had children all over the British Isles...'

'[She was] intensely religious of the fire & brimstone era, yet she bought & sold many pubs. Her modus operandi [was] to station 'the husband' outside to count how many people passed before she bought, to build up & sell.'

Tales of sixteen children may be over the top, but there is no reason to doubt the basics of Ena's story. She tells us that Louisa put some sort of 'dowry' from her parents into the gymnastics business. The Woodwards' licensed victualling was prospering in 1864, so it could have been quite a substantial sum.

Ena describes Charles and Louisa's early lifestyle as 'very posh'. They settled in Bryantwood Road, Islington, not far from what is now the Emirates, Arsenal Football Club's stadium. The family, which eventually included five sons and two daughters, was not always to live in such pleasant surroundings.

Charles Spencer exploited the gymnastic craze further with the publication of his first book, *The Modern Gymnast: being practical instructions on the horizontal bar, parallel bars, vaulting horse, flying trapeze etc*, in 1866, the year after the opening of the German Gymnasium. The title page describes him as 'Charles Spencer, Professor of Gymnastics'. The book boasts one hundred and twenty practical illustrations, together with detailed instructions.

Naturally, Snoxell and Spencer, 'manufacturers of every description of portable and fixed gymnastic apparatus', advertised in the endpapers of Charles' book. The 'Compound Chest Machine', their most expensive offering at £50, was 'a most highly finished and effective gymnastic contrivance, containing upwards of 100 different exercises... It is invaluable in Hospitals and Schools (more especially Ladies') and large Families'. The large families would have to have been well off: £50 was almost double a labourer's annual wage. You could have a vaulting horse at a more reasonable price (£8-£12 depending on size).

The introduction makes clear that Charles was not going to pad his handbook with ancient history lessons:

'I shall merely note the revival of gymnastics in our own times, which began in Germany, and was consequent, we are told, upon the spirit of resistance evoked by the conquests of the first French empire.'

Worries about French military power sound strange today when television persistently replays stories of when the Germans were European bad guys. But French aggression haunted English nineteenth century minds. Many people, like Charles' parents, remembered the invasion threats of the Napoleonic Wars only too well.

Those fears were renewed after January 14th, 1858, when Felice Orsini threw a bomb under the carriage of Emperor Napoleon III and his Empress as it was drawing up at the door of a Paris theatre. They were unhurt, but when it became clear that Orsini had tested his bombs in the English countryside, a hundred French colonels signed a petition to the Emperor, demanding that he lead them against England.

In the panic, English campaigners for a volunteer rifle corps, a sort of Territorial Army, found they were pushing at an open door. On May 12th 1859 the Government sent a circular to the Lords Lieutenant of every county establishing the Volunteers.

Alfred Tennyson encouraged men to the colours with a poem in *The Times* which included the lines

> *'Ready, be ready to meet the storm!*
> *Rifleman, rifleman, rifleman form!'*

Despite the Poet Laureate's contribution, recruitment was rapid. One almanac suggests that over 190,000 men were enrolled that year. The Volunteers were to have appropriate standards of training and service. They marched, drilled, practised rifle marksmanship, and, most significantly for Snoxell and Spencers' sales figures, paraded regularly for gymnastics training all over England.

The Emperor of France shushed his over-excited colonels and the threat of invasion was removed. But the Volunteers continued to flourish, as did the volume of their requisitions for gymnastic equipment and physical training.

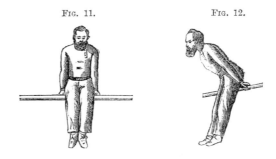

fig. 22. The 'sit-swing' illustrated in the Modern Gymnast

The thoroughness of Charles' manual reminds me of the detail in his father's notes on balloon-making. It teaches you every exercise from 'throwing somersaults' to the 'Hindu punishment or muscle grind'. Charles says:

'I have just jotted down the following descriptive remarks; being well aware, at the same time of the difficulty of teaching anything of the kind on paper, but in the hope they may be useful to those who really wish to improve themselves; and with the wish that the taste for these manly recreations may rapidly spread.'

'In the forward sit-swing, the first start is the principal thing , as the impetus gained will be sufficient, to bring you again. In order to get a good start, you must bring the body as far away from the bar as possible, supporting the whole weight on the arms, as in in Fig.11;now throw the chest out and the head back, with legs rather straight, then with a good plunge forward, keeping the arms straight as in Fig.12, you will go quite round. That is to say, you will in time, for you must not think of succeeding at first in any of these feats, but perseverance will soon enable you to accomplish them.'

Gymnastics was largely a male preserve, like many other activities in Victorian England. But women were increasingly expected to practise it while they were young; and girls' schools were often equipped with gymnastic apparatus. Authors inveighed against lack of exercise:

'Practically the whole of the ailments to which young girls are subject can be traced to the [faulty and unnatural school routine]. It is considered ladylike to be very quiet and demure, to take little or no

exercise, lace tightly while the body is still developing; graceful, to sit or stand in certain prescribed positions, take short steps while walking; but we lose sight of that all this is detrimental to health and quite unnatural. …the higher the social position the more the instincts are crushed.'

The Modern Gymnast describes Charles' visits to oversee the fitting of sets of equipment. He enjoyed showing off, as he tells us in his account of a trip to a 'large school'.

'…the boys, knowing me to be a gymnast, requested me to oblige them with a specimen of what could immediately be done in that way. This of course I immediately did, and showed them a few of the advanced exercises on the horizontal bar and parallels, to the immense delight of the pupils, but also to the intense horror of the instructor, who considered them too dangerous for them to attempt.'

'About three weeks afterwards I had occasion to go there again, when rather to my surprise, I found that nearly all the boys could do the feats I had shown them on the previous occasion; and they begged me to show them some more of my 'jolly exercises' as they somewhat irreverently termed them, saying, "Oh! there is no amusement in what professor So-and-so shows us, stupid hand-over-the-hand exercises under the bar; we really begin to think that he cannot do anything else.'

Professor So-and So's view of the incident might not have been so jolly.

Charles tells us that he was teased for his painstaking approach to new exercises and that he could perform every one of those shown in the book. Illustrations ram the point home by showing a bearded figure in graceful motion on bars, trapeze and rings. Charles' beard became symbolically important to the aeronautical firm he later founded. His son Percy grew a beard when he took over 'because the workers expected it'.

Further European travels brought new commercial opportunities. He learned the handspring with 'a clever acrobat in Paris'. Charles makes clear that when he first became involved, English vaulting horses were poorly designed and dangerous. He brought a German design back for Snoxell and Spencer to manufacture: it has remained the standard pattern ever since.

This first book seems to have been a success. Charles carried on writing and publishing for the rest of his life, but never wrote anything substantial about aeronautics, though heavily involved in early experiments.

During June 1868, the Great Hall of the Crystal Palace held the first exhibition of the Aeronautical Society. Here you could see such marvels as Stringfellow's steam-driven flying machine along with kites, miniature engines and spring-driven ornithopters. Model balloons hung in the air.

Outside in the grounds, Charles Spencer was giving his own show, running and gliding in his flying machine. The patent for the machine describes it as 'An improved apparatus or machine or machine for enabling persons to support, raise and propel themselves through the air, which apparatus, when fitted with suitable mechanism and raised, is also self-propelling.' The last bit sounds a bit optimistic, but the 'aeroplane' was certainly advanced for the time.

E. Charles Vivian says:

'Charles Spencer [was] the first man to practise gliding in England. His apparatus consisted of a pair of wings with a total area of 30 sq. ft., to which a tail and body were attached. The weight of this apparatus was some 24 lbs., and, launching himself on it from a small eminence, as was done later by Lilienthal in his experiments, the inventor made flights of over 120 feet.'

Charles' first aerial experiments came to an end with his gliding successes. But he would, some years afterwards, return to aeronautics.

fig. 23. George Spencer and velocipede. The date is more likely to be 1869

• IV •

Enter the velocipede

As if gymnastics and aeronautics were not enough, Snoxell and Spencer Ltd was soon able to surf yet another craze. The velocipede or 'boneshaker', the earliest practical bicycle, was about to cross the channel. Stories of its arrival are confused: Nick Clayton and John Green of the Veteran-Cycle Club kindly guided my path through the maze.

David Herlihy explains in *Bicycle* that Rowley Turner was a young businessman who saw early versions of the velocipede in Paris and encouraged his uncle, Josiah Turner, who manufactured sewing machines in Coventry, that they should build large numbers of velocipedes. Turner's partners in Paris were Pascaud et Cie, who sold you the Coventry-built machines they imported and taught you to ride them in their gymnasium.

England was well behind France in the bicycle business. John Mayall says that he saw his first velocipede in England in January 1869. Rowley Turner, who had travelled from Paris with the machine, demonstrated its possibilities in Spencers' Gymnasium in Old Street. His skill impressed Mayall.

'We were some half dozen spectators, and I shall never forget our astonishment at the sight of Mr Turner whirling himself round the room, sitting on a bar above a pair of wheels that ought, as we innocently supposed, to fall down immediately he jumped off the ground. Judge then our greater surprise when instead of stopping by tilting sideways on to one foot, he slowly halted and turning the front wheel diagonally remained quite still, balancing on the wheels!'

'I turned to Mr Spencer and exclaimed, "By Jove, Charley, there's a balance!"'

Turner kept his demonstration going a little longer, gave them a short talk on how to cycle and left them to it. The account makes clear that this was Charles Spencer's own machine, ordered from Turner. As soon as Turner had left, Spencer leaped onto the velocipede. They spent the evening trying out the new toy. Mayall was hooked.

FIG. 1.

HOW TO COMMENCE PRACTICE.

FIG. 3.

HOW TO GET ON BY THE TREADLE.

FIG. 4.

HOW TO ALIGHT.

FIG. 5.

TO RIDE SIDE-SADDLE.

FIG. 7.

RIDING WITHOUT USING THE HANDS.

FIG. 10.

fig. 24. Illustrations from Charles Spencer (1866) The Modern Bicycle

'I may say in all candour that I was fairly enamoured of the Velocipede.'

He came back at 6 am the following morning for another practice session.

Mayall and Spencer saw the machine as a new piece of gymnastic equipment:

'for example, while I was riding around, Mr Spencer mounted my shoulders and made grotesque poses; he tried to stand on his hands on my shoulders, and not being quite equal to the feat he toppled over and upset me; we thus got one of our earliest experiences of the sort of exercises to which the Velocipede did not lend itself kindly.'

Spencer's fall stopped him practising much the following day, but nothing could keep Mayall from his new passion. They took the velocipede to Regents Park on a cab and Mayall tried a few quick rides down the paths. An outraged park-keeper came after them, 'waving a stick in closer proximity than I quite approved.' They retreated to Mayall's house in Adelaide Road, Camden. After refreshment it was time to move on. Charles managed a few short runs down a hill, but generally provided moral support.

'His cheerfulness, his shouts of encouragement when I succeeded in bowling along for a minute or two without halt, the willingness with which he helped in every way-all buoyed up my flagging strength till we reached his house. We dragged the machine into the garden, and I staggered onto a sofa and lay there some minutes in an exhausted state.'

By next day Mayall was recovered and pedalled down Goswell Road to 'a mighty cheer from the crowd that struck me as being quite as much derisive as of encouragement.' Far from being put off, he was becoming increasingly ambitious.

Mayall explains that he cycled to a friend's house in Clapham. He stayed the night and next day, full of pioneering energy, managed to ride to Redhill 20 miles south. He came back to London by train with the velocipede in the guard's van and arrived at Spencers' Gymnasium when it was 'quite dark. …they were all very anxious to know what had become of me and the machine.'

Mayall says he then 'spoke to Mr Spencer of my intention of trying to reach Brighton in a day. He fell in with it with hearty enthusiasm and said he would like to go with me.' Mayall is being a little disingenuous. All those involved knew that the velocipede was hot property. For example, *The Ironmonger* of January 30th 1869 noted 'The mere fact that we have not yet experienced the furore that has accompanied the introduction of the iron horse into France, constitutes no evidence that it will not be equally popular in this country.'

The Ironmonger was right. The London to Brighton ride was the turning point in English public awareness of the velocipede, and almost certainly planned as such. To hype the event, the partners persuaded a London *Times* reporter called Collins to travel behind the riders. His account was syndicated to 400 local papers.

Spencer's workshops, according to Mayall's account in the *Ixion*, only turned out two copies of the original machine. Charles confirmed this version of events in his *Bicycles and Tricycles*:

'It was at first proposed that they [the velocipedes] should be manufactured at my works in London, but finding that it would be impossible to manufacture them quickly enough, it was decided to give an order to the Coventry Machinists' Company whose extensive works and suitable machinery at Cheylesmore would enable them to furnish as many as might be required.'

So the real story is that Snoxell and Spencer became the English retail agency for the Coventry Machinists Company. They sold the velocipedes with the same choice of models as Turner offered in Paris.

'The first order was for 500 of the new two-wheeled velocipedes at £8 each, of which 250 were to be sent to Paris and 250 to me in London.'

One Snoxell and Spencer trade-marked velocipede in good condition survives in the Canterbury Museum. The technical details are intriguing. The newspaper photograph of George Spencer (see page 40) shows that that the velocipede had a rear brake line that ran up to the handlebars for tightening. The line went up through a hole in the centre of the handlebars. To brake, you twisted the handlebars hard. It was straightforward but may not have been wonderfully effective.

The velocipede has a front wheel of wood with a metal rim; the back wheel is metal. You could not freewheel without taking your feet off the pedals, so the bicyclist is provided with footrests above the level of the front wheel. So you can freewheel downhill, raising the feet from the pedals and putting them high on the foot rests in a pose rather similar to that sometimes adopted for gynaecological examination. A flock of Victorian gentlemen freewheeling down a hill with their legs in the air must have given joy to spectators.

FIG. 6.   FIG. 8.

TO REST THE LEGS.   RIDING WITHOUT USING LEGS OR HANDS.

fig. 25. Taking it easy: suggestions from The Modern Bicycle

At that time there was at least the possibility of competition. *The Field* reported a two man two mile velocipede race in Dulwich at the end of January 1869. We also know that an enterprising saddler named A. Davis had started advertising velocipedes before Snoxell and Spencer; he published a bicycle training manual and put an advertisement in the *English Mechanic* on the 12th February 1869.

But neither development prompted the public response that Turner and Snoxell and Spencer achieved. When Rowley Turner, John Mayall jr and Charles Spencer rode a lap of honour round Trafalgar Square before heading off to Brighton on the 17th February 1869 they were surrounded by a huge crowd. As we shall see, the three men were probably riding the original Turner-imported machine and the two Spencer copies.

From that point spin has probably muddied the truth about the ride. The different accounts kept the correspondence columns of *The Boneshaker* bouncing for several months. By the end of the exchanges at least one column had appeared headed 'Mr Spencer's Pork Pies'.

A Snoxell and Spencer advertisement appeared in the *English Mechanic* and *Mirror of Science* of the nineteenth of February 1869, two days after the ride:

'The New Two-Wheel Velocipede

Messrs. Snoxell and Spencer, Velocipede and Gymnastic Apparatus Manufacturers, having introduced the best Paris model of The New Two-Wheel Velocipede, and having made several important improvements thereon, are now prepared to execute orders to any extent.

The Velocipedes now offered are made of the best materials throughout; they are well tested, and admit of the greatest speed, with the least exertion, that have yet been offered to the public.

Purchasers can have instruction, by proficient performers, in their large Practice Room and on that Velocipede most suitable to the purchaser. Gentlemen are invited to inspect them in use at Messrs. S. and S.'s[sic] Factory and Practice Room, 35 Old-street, St.Luke's.'

The advertisement then includes a long quote from *The Times* of February 19th 1869:

On Wednesday, Mr John Mayall jun., son of the well known photographer, Mr Charles Spencer (Snoxell and Spencer) and Mr Turner, accomplished the journey from London to Brighton, each on one of Snoxell and Spencer's new two wheeled velocipedes.

After a preliminary run round Trafalgar Square, they started off at the rate of eight miles an hour on roads which proved to be generally good against a strong head wind all the way.

They kept pretty close together as far as Crawley (thirty miles) and then Mr Mayall took a decided lead and arrived at Brighton, his companions well up in time, in good condition for dinner and the second part of 'Ku'he' concert at the Grand Hall. Part of the journey down from Clayton to Brighton was run at the speed of one mile in four minutes.'

The Spencers liked this quotation from *The Times* so much that an almost identical version appears in their advertising right through the next thirty years.

At the end of the 1990s the historians of the Veteran-Cycling Club began to pick away at this version of events. Bob George looked up the original report in The Times which included:

'They kept pretty well together as far as Crawley (thirty miles) and then Mr Mayall took a decided lead and arrived at Brighton, in good condition for dinner and the second part of Ku'he's concert at the Grand Hall.'

Then John Liffen, another VCC investigator, went to the British Newspaper Library in London and found this hardly subedited version in the *Brighton Examiner*, one of the 400 papers to which the original *Times* article was syndicated. 'They kept pretty well together as far as Crawley (thirty miles) where Mr Mayall's friends gave up on account of the difficulty experienced in running against the strong wind.'

As John Liffen says '…there is no reason why the *Brighton Examiner*'s report should be relied on more than any others. However, its inclusion of the specific detail about Turner and Spencer giving up does give it the ring of authority.'

So perhaps Charles Spencer, or his brother George, concealed the fact that he and Turner never made it to Brighton on their velocipedes. As the *Ixion* article makes clear, Rowley

Turner was an excellent rider. Lack of skill seems unlikely to have stopped him reaching Brighton, even in a headwind.

We might guess that John Mayall was riding his favourite imported velocipede and that it held together all the way. The others would have been riding the Spencer–made copies, which perhaps succumbed to the stress of the journey. It is not surprising that Snoxell and Spencers preferred the doctored version.

Whatever the truth, the campaign for the velocipede was well and truly launched. George Spencer's 1909 interview paints a picture of bicycle mania:

'We had hundreds of flaming posters put up all over the place and boomed the new machines for all they were worth.

Our success was astonishing. Streams of people poured in and out of our shop all day long, and rows of cabs stood outside. We took as much as £90 a day during that period, and gave lessons at 2s 6d a piece [in the Gymnasium] to those who bought machines. They cost us about £5.15s to make. We could make one of them in about two days and sell it easily for £10.

Our first customers were Stock Exchange men, who went in for the new sport keenly. Charles Dickens, too, was one of the buyers, and he was immensely pleased with his purchase. He said it diverted his thoughts to ride about the country on it.

We sold hundreds of machines for two or three years, and then the Germans started making imitations so cheap and bad that they fell to pieces after a very little wear. That gave all boneshakers a bad name and the trade was ruined.'

Much of this is in the Spencer copy-writing tradition. Snoxell and Spencer only manufactured two velocipedes, as far as we know; Charles Dickens was on his last legs by 1869 and in no state to ride a velocipede, though he could have bought one. Whether or not the Germans were turning out cheap copies, something happened much nearer home that took the Coventry Machinists Company licence away from Snoxell and Spencer.

But the overall picture presented by George Spencer is accurate. The mania is well-documented. It was a boom time for velocipede merchants and Snoxell and Spencer had a extraordinary few months. Sales poured in from all over the country.

For example, the *South Durham Herald* reported: 'Several members of the Hartlepool Phoenix Club recently formed themselves into a velocipede club… On Thursday, Mr Atley, deputed by the other members, proceeded to Newcastle, in order to purchase a velocipede of the bicycle make from Messrs Snoxell and Spencer. In consequence of the great demand which at present exists, he was unable to procure one; but orders were given for one of a very good description-the price being £12-which, it is expected, will arrive at Hartlepool during the course of the ensuing week.' (The prices depended on the size of the front wheel. The standard wheel model at 32 inches high was £10; the most expensive at £14 was a version with a 48 inch front wheel.)

The 1860s seemed set to end in triumph, fame and prosperity for everyone associated with Snoxell and Spencer. It was not to be. A colossal family row led Charles to leave the firm in November 1869 and the partnership was formally broken.

George Spencer, as older brother, was always going to become managing director when his uncle died. Perhaps Charles, who was better known to the public than George, felt his position did not suit his renown.

Changes in the cycle business by 1870 may also have put the firm's finances under stress. The technology was moving ahead. New manufacturers were emerging from the old monolithic companies. For example, several ex-employees from the Coventry Machinists' Company had struck out to set up their own businesses.

fig. 26. Charles Spencer's catalogue: the attempt to go it alone

Or perhaps something darker was going on at Snoxell and Spencer. Ena, his grand-daughter, recounted Charles' version in her notes on the family. 'He [Charles] found his brother 'great uncle George' cheating. They were in business, manufacturing gymnastic apparatus. Angrily he broke with George and got cheated out of everything, including Grandma's sizeable dowry which was invested in the business.'

Charles quickly set up his own business and issued an eight page catalogue: 'Charles Spencer, Manufacturer of Gymnastic Apparatus, Velocipedes and Athletic and British Sport Requirements. Contractor of Gymnasia to Her Majesty's Army'. The catalogue is full of 'requisites': fencing requisites, athletic requisites and velocipede requisites alongside items required for British sports, including footballs and cricket bats. And of course £10 or £12 velocipedes were available.

But the firm failed: Charles was declared bankrupt in January 1871. Though he, Louisa and the family were still in their house in Bryantwood Road at the time of the census in April 1871, they soon had to move house to Ringcroft Street, a less desirable part of Islington. Ena tells us that 'Grandma Woodward brought them the house in Ringcroft Street.' Grandma Woodward was, of course, the specialist investor in run-down public houses.

MR. THOMAS SPARROW.

fig. 27. Thomas Sparrow

THE BICYCLE TRIP FROM LONDON TO JOHN O'GROAT'S

fig. 28. The London to John o'Groats team: Charles Spencer is on the left

After the divorce

George and Charles Spencers' paths diverged completely after 1870. Neither brother mentions the other in any surviving communication after that date.

Charles found his way forward through partnership with Thomas Dutton Templer Sparrow. Frederick and Anne Sparrow, Thomas' parents, lived near the childhood home of Diana, Charles' mother. Frederick Sparrow was convicted of public nuisance in 1815 when fumes of his gas works right next door to the Snoxells in Dorset Street, near Fleet Street, stank out the neighbourhood. He eventually sorted out the smell and it all calmed down.

Thomas Sparrow went into brushmaking and in the 1861 census describes himself as employing 'seven hands'. By 1870 the business may not have been making much money: the price of ivory, the traditional material for the backs of brushes, was high and celluloid, which was to replace it, was only just coming in.

So family contacts may have been involved when in 1871 Thomas Sparrow picked up Charles Spencer and, with him, the contract as retail agent for the Coventry Machinists' Company bicycles. Charles was always more involved with velocipedes than the others in the family firm. He may have walked out with an understanding from the Coventry Machinists on Sparrow's takeover of the contract.

The new partnership had premises in Knightsbridge and Piccadilly. *The Survey of London* reports that 'Thomas Sparrow, bicycle maker and agent for the Coventry Machinists Company Ltd, and the firm of Sparrow & Spencer, manufacturers of gymnastic apparatus and government contractors for military gymnasia, occupied these premises, known as No. 21A High Road [in Knightsbridge Green], for several years in the early and mid-1870s (at which time they also had a shop in Piccadilly).'

The National Museum of Scotland has an example of the machines Sparrow was selling in the early 1870s identified by a brass plate marked 'SPARROW MAKER 89 PICCADILLY'.

The partnership only took out one patent and it has Charles' fingerprints all over it: it was

fig. 29. Charles Spencer in later life

for 'a new or improved boomerang, and mechanical apparatus for propelling or projecting the same'. This fantastical invention never flew; or if it did, it went, returned and vanished without making any impact on 1870s London.

The company organised a pioneering journey from London to John o'Groats in 1873. According to *Bicycling News* the trip was paid for by Thomas Sparrow as 'the first of those long journeys which have perhaps more than anything else to attract public attention to the bicycle as a road machine, and demonstrated to the general public, who previously doubted its value, that the modern two-wheeler is a thoroughly trustworthy aid in touring operations.'

Sparrow had been introducing solid rubber tyres to replace the early iron-rimmed ones. 'The English were very busy building railroads, ships, and empires, so that not much attention was given to Sparrow. By 1873, however, he had got a following, and he financed a great 1,000 mile run from Land's End to John o' Groats. Sparrow also rode a wheel most of the way with them, taking careful note of the behavior of the different machines, in order to discover and remedy their weak points.'

Fifteen cyclists met up in the Middlesex Bicycle Club Room in the Kings Arms Hotel, Kensington on the 2nd June, 1873. In *The Modern Bicycle*, Charles Spencer describes how after 'a capital breakfast' the party set out together. The object of the trip, he says, was to gather 'some idea of the distance that could be travelled on a bicycle without preliminary training, and on the ordinary turnpike roads... ' They cycled up Park Lane, then through London's 'muddy roads' out to Archway and up the Great North Road, making their way through Potters Bar, Welwyn, to Baldock, where they stopped, probably at about 2pm, for dinner. After dinner, most of the party cycled back down to London, covering, as the Secretary of the Middlesex Bicycle Club could point out with pride, 'eighty miles in the day'.

Five cyclists, including Charles Spencer and Thomas Sparrow, pressed on to Biggleswade where they stopped 'to oil their machines' near a Whit Monday fair and 'the country folks manifested the greatest interest and excitement.' The cyclists were riding machines with a variety of wheel sizes: their front wheels ranged from 52 inches to 45 inches in diameter, so there was certainly something to look at. Then the party swept on to Buckden, sixty miles from London, where they spent the night.

The next day brought little excitement until they reached Nottinghamshire. Here they were first soaked by a torrent of rain and then assaulted by a drunk. 'I am sorry to have to say that 5 miles from Newark we met an intoxicated yokel driving a half-broken horse, and one of our party, who was behind, kindly vaulted off his bicycle to allow more room to pass; in return for which the bumpkin got down from his trap and quite unexpectedly and unprovokedly knocked the bicyclist down, giving his opinion that " such d...d things should not be allowd." As it was considered of great importance that the trip should not be interrupted, it was considered better not to have any altercation, especially in the beery state in which the man was, and... he was allowed to go on his way...'.

The party trundled on determinedly for the next four days, making slower time than planned because of headwinds and rain. Thomas Sparrow left the party at Durham and went to London to look after the business, which should have gained sales from all the publicity surrounding the ride.

They stopped for the night at Alnwick. The riders were now near the Border and enjoying the quality of the road surfaces, though the wind was still fierce. They reached Edinburgh next day. 'We must have presented a curious spectacle, the road being dry and very dusty, and as we were naturally in a state of moisture from the great exertion of battling against a strong wind, the dust adhered to our faces and formed a complete mask.' It was a poor day by their standards: only 30 miles were covered.

On the following day, with guidance from a local cyclist, Mr Forsyth, they took the ferry over the Firth of Forth and set off towards the Highlands. Charles warns travellers to take their own food on any trip through the Highlands. They had high hopes at Dalwhinnie where 'a good inn… was shown on the maps'…'but, alas for vanity of human wishes!' It had shut 'in consequence of the opening of the Highland Railway, and consequent diversion of the traffic.' They made do with 'oatcake and milk from a shepherd's hut', which hardly scratched the surface of what a Victorian cyclist expected for his dinner. But the scenery was terrific and the undernourished heroes struggled on to Kingussie. On the following day, they managed forty miles through 'barren and mountainous' country which was soon almost blotted out by thick 'Scotch mist', soft persistent rain, which soaked them to the skin.

But it all turned out all right. The landlord of the Moy Inn where they stopped for the night produced 'his stock of wearables and placed them freely at our service.' Charles liked dressing up. Ena tells us he always wore a frock coat [and was] high hatted and suave'. So that evening he arrayed himself in 'full Highland costume of velvet coat, kilt, sporran etc, etc.'

On the thirteenth day the weather remained awful. On the fourteenth, June 15th, they had a long wait for the Mickle Ferry on Dornock Firth and then had a pub lunch to which Charles awarded a grudging one star: 'I should not advise anyone to put faith in it for anything more than bread and cheese, with a glass of whisky or beer'.

On their fifteenth and last day, the cyclists faced the ascent of the Ord of Caithness-and its descent: …so steep, that for the first time, we were obliged to descend from our trusty machines and wheel them for some distance down the decline.'

After that, everything improved dramatically. 'The whole population' of Wick met them as they entered the town, 'making quite an afternoon's holiday, flags and banners waving on all sides.' They had dinner at the New Inn and then pushed on for the final eighteen miles to John o' Groats and a warm welcome, complete with lobster supper, from Mr and Mrs McKenzie of the famous Huna Inn. 'The Huna Inn… with its tonic air which brought you waves of dreamless sleep and an appetite – well – the Huna with the ships so close under your window you could hear the sailors talk'.

Eventually a wagonette took the riders and their velocipedes back to Wick for the night. Next day they made their triumphant return by steamer to Aberdeen and then by train on to London. They had covered 800 miles, said Charles. The journey via Berwick is probably nearer 680 miles. But they had done it in 14 days, at approximately 48 miles a day in often terrible weather and headwinds, on rather primitive machines.

The journey was a huge success in terms of column inches in the press. Mr Lucas, the Secretary of the Middlesex Bicycle Club, and Thomas Sparrow easily swatted away an attack in *The Field* by someone calling himself *Qui vive*, who was peddling (or pedalling?) the story that Sparrow had broken 'the backbone' of his bicycle in Durham and come back for that reason. Sparrow insisted that not one of his bicycles 'turned out over the last three years had had its backbone broken.' Lucas argued that 'representatives of the local press' watched the machines 'from town to town the whole of the distance, thus leaving no room for misrepresentation.' That seems to have been the end of that.

But the partnership did not last. Thomas Sparrow and Charles Spencer dissolved it in 1875 with Sparrow taking responsibility for all their debts. Charles had decided to try his hand at magazine publishing. The first issue of *Ixion, A Magazine of Velocipeding, Athletics and Aerostatics* appeared in January 1875. As we have seen, its 45 pages included John Mayall's 'Recollection of the first days of the bicycle'. Mayall wrote a follow-up for the second *Ixion* in February and Spencer kept the show on the road for three more issues. But the May issue was the last.

Perhaps Charles was trying too hard: he was editor, reporter and banker to the magazine

('Cheques and Post-Office Orders should be made payable to Charles Green'). Perhaps *Ixion* skimmed too many areas: the March issue contained items on bicycles, athletics, football, rowing, yachting, swimming and hockey. Perhaps Charles had made enemies. His curt dismissal of a clergyman, 'Rev. E.P.M', who wrote to the editor suggesting cycling as a sport for women, will have won few friends in progressive circles: 'We do not agree with you that the bicycle is a suitable kind of exercise for ladies.' Charles suggests that ladies should take themselves to the gymnastic classes run for them at the German Gymnastic Society. Whatever the causes, the *Ixion* was history and Charles had to move on again.

He remained active in the world of cycling right through the 1870s and wrote twelve books on the bicycle and bicycling. *The Modern Bicycle* appeared when the market had moved on to what we know as the 'penny farthing'. Charles gives illustrated instructions (the bearded expert is back in action), on such essential topics as 'Putting your feet on the treadles.'

The section explains how to mount 'a saddle nearly as high as your shoulder' and advice on starting to wobble forward.

'At this time pay strict attention to the steering, and take care never to let go one hand until you have a firm grasp with the other, or you and the whole affair may come to extreme grief.'

Health tips are included: the superbiker should 'have a cold or tepid-bath daily' and 'Vegetables and stimulants in great moderation are now allowed…'

Charles also persevered with gymnastic equipment manufacture. The Spencer brothers competed with one another in the Post Office commercial directory of 1880.

'Spencer Charles and Co (of the original firm Snoxell and Spencer) manufacturers of gymnastic apparatus and sole contractors to HM War dept for military gymnasia & makers of all requisites for British sports; manufacturers of patent revolving shutters in wood or iron; 2 Old St, corner of Goswell Rd'

'Spencer, George (late Snoxell and Spencer established 98 years) also maker of gymnastic apparatus to HRH Prince of Wales, the British Army and the London, Croydon, Hornsey, Nottingham & Newmarket School Boards, 385 Old Street & 52 Goswell Rd EC, near Aldersgate St station.'

It was really no contest. George had the factory, the Snoxell capital and the contacts in England and abroad. His life had settled into a pattern. He married Kate Coleman, daughter of a Clerkenwell baker, on the 4th December 1869, just before the family row. He described himself as an 'engineer' on the marriage certificate. Kate was twenty two and was living with her brother Joseph in New North Road, Islington; George lived just round the corner in Packington Street. Kate walked back down the aisle a head above her new husband, who, while a famously fit gymnast, had inherited the Spencers' short stature.

George needed to be competent. Uncle William Snoxell favoured an exceptionally leisurely work-life balance. His daily routine involved a brief visit to the firm before lunch, a short walk home and an afternoon with his mechanical toys and automata. 'His rooms were full of them, and after doing two hours business in the morning he would go home to Charterhouse Square and play with his 'gimcracks' as he called them, for the rest of the day. One of his toys, I remember, was a lifesize lady who played the piano when you wound her up. There were dozens of clockwork birds in cages, which chirruped when the key was turned, and clocks by the score. We found 250 of them in his rooms when he died and they realised £2000 at auction. One of the clocks had a mechanism that was supposed to have solved the problem of perpetual motion. I myself knew it for seven or eight years and it never stopped in my time.' The Puttick and Simpson auctioneers' catalogue of June 1879 survives in the Guildhall Library. The lots advertised include 'mechanical automata, musical instruments, paintings, clocks and watches and other objects of art'.

MAYALL, Photo. LONDON & BRIGHTON

MAYALL, Photo. LONDON & BRIGHTON

fig. 30–31. George Cuvier Spencer (left) and his wife Kate, nee Coleman (right)

So George had had plenty of practice by the time he became managing director after William's death in 1879 . He renamed the company George Spencer and Co and, with name changes as partners joined or left the board, it ran successfully for nearly one hundred years. George was now, at 46, running a substantial small business. The 1881 census does not mention gymnastics equipment, though it was a substantial part of the business, but records George as 'a house and shop fittings shutter manufacturer, employing 17 men and 3 boys'. George employed a servant to help Kate with the house and their four young children.

The firm expanded at home and internationally through the 1880s. One advertisement listed the awards:

By Special Appointment to the Governor-General of Canada and HM Queen
1883 Rio de Janeiro Educational Congress Highest Award
1884 International Health Exhibition Prize
1886 International Exhibition Liverpool Highest Award
1888 Danish Exhibition Gold Medal
1897 Gold Medal Brussels Exhibition-only award

This was the perfect time to be in the sports business: 'At the beginning of the 1890s, London was both the heart of intercontinental Europe and the capital of modern sports, both amateur and professional. From the continental sporting viewpoint, British sporting authority was unquestionable, because the UK was advanced in many sports, and these were duly registered, studied, commented on and perfected. Moreover, it was seen as compulsory for continental professional athletes to visit London.' *The Gymnast* magazine summed up the situation in *Modern Life* in October 1893.

Visitor – to son of house – Is your father at home?
S No, he is out skating.
V But your sister is at home?
S She is at the Fencing class.
V And your mother?
S She is training for the Long Distance Walk.
V The Cook is at home, I presume?
S She has gone to exercise her lungs at the Salvation Army Hall.
V Well then, I suppose I must wait here till someone comes home, if you do not mind.
S Oh, yes, I do mind, I am going to the Gymnasium.

In contrast to George's prosperous lifestyle, money remained an issue for Charles. Ena asks in her reminiscences, 'Have you heard of the lean days when the shopkeepers used to beg him [Charles] to do tricks, sleight of hand, "Please, Mr Spencer" with eggs & Grandpa used to keep the egg supply up at home?'

The 1881 census gives some idea of the pressure on Louise, Charles' wife, who is by then looking after five boys and two girls, with no live-in servant mentioned. Only two oldest boys, Percival and Arthur, are in work and the youngest, Sydney, is just one year old.

Charles made a small income from his *Cycling Road Book*. (The series continued after his death. The publisher, Grube, updated the book as *The Cyclists and Automobilists Roadbook*, by Charles Spencer, in 1904.) But others dominated the bicycle sales business where the real money was.

It was time for Charles to embark on a new career.

BALLOONS TO CARRY PASSENGERS.

Balloon of 20,000 cubic feet capacity, of the best Balloon fabric, Italian hemp netting,
improved valve, basket car, grapnell, with ropes, and forty ballast bags, ascending
power equal to two passengers and 2 cwt. ballast ....   Price £130

Ditto of 30,000 cubic feet capacity, ascending power equal to three passengers, and
proportionate weight of ballast   ....   Price £150

Ditto of 40,000 cubic feet capacity, five passengers ....   Price £175

Ditto of 60,000 cubic feet capacity, seven passengers....   ....   Price £200

*Special quotations for Silk or Skin Balloons of the above or greater
capacity. Also War Balloons of every description.*

Balloon Ascents		Scientific Ascents
Throughout the Country,		**CONDUCTED**
FOR		
FETES, GALAS,		Juvenile Balloon Races,
Private and Public		for Fetes,
EXHIBITIONS,		Galas, Garden Parties,
Garden & Pleasure Parties.		&c.
TERMS POST FREE.		*ESTIMATES GIVEN.*

CHARLES GREEN SPENCER & SON'S
PATENT ASBESTOS MONTGOLFIER BALLOON,
FOR WAR PURPOSES.

Up to the present time it has been generally accepted that Gas was the only means by which Balloons could be inflated; for, though the original idea of Montgolfier was to inflate them by means of rarefied air, created by combustion at the neck of the Balloon, still the danger attending the experiments, when the Balloon was made of combustible materials, was so great that it rendered the use of Fire Balloons utterly impracticable. Montgolfier's theory was doubtless correct, and, provided the Balloon itself can be rendered incombustible, the advantages of the one inflated by rarefied air over the one inflated by gas, are sufficiently manifest, and this cannot be more clearly demonstrated than in the case of an army acting in a hostile country. It would there be impossible to carry about or obtain a sufficient quantity of gas to inflate a Balloon, and even if, after a long and intricate process, the gas could be manufactured, the time required for inflation would be several hours. But in a Fire-proof Balloon sufficient heat to raise it may be obtained in a few minutes, as has been demonstrated in the recent experiments under the inspection of the Royal Engineers' Committee, Chatham, and at the Welsh Harp, Hendon. So that, for war purposes, or for an exploring expedition, an ascent may be accomplished without any trouble, at very little expense, and without any encumbrances connected with the ordinary Gas Balloon.

In addition to the above advantages, the difference between the expense of inflating one by gas and that of inflating one by means of rarefied air is vastly in favour of the latter.

The danger is diminished in a corresponding proportion; for, the large volume of gas in an ordinary Balloon is in itself deleterious; whereas the rarefied air in a Fire-proof Balloon is absolutely harmless, being capable of being raised or lowered as required, by the simple process of turning the spirit lamp at the neck a little up or down.

In short, the Asbestos Patent Balloon, composed of Asbestos Cloth in the lower part, and of lighter, but thoroughly uninflammable materials, in every other part, possesses advantages which must commend themselves to every scientific and practical persons interested in the question.

CHARLES GREEN SPENCER.

NOTE.—These, like all other Captive Balloons, can only be used during Calm Weather.
The Russian Government has adopted these Balloons for War purposes.

fig. 32. C.G.Spencer & Son handbill, probably from the early 1880s

C.G. Spencer & Sons

Charles Spencer had inherited one important resource: his father's notes on balloon-building. So he started making balloons in a new firm, C.G.Spencer & Son of Highbury. The 'son' was Percival, who had made his first balloon ascent with his father from Crystal Palace at the age of eight. Percy had technical education at Cowper Street College off City Road, Islington.

The business probably opened in late 1881. The firm patented the Spencer Brothers Asbestos (Montgolfier) fire [hot air] balloon in 1882. C.G. Spencer and Son set out to be an aeronautical one stop shop, designer emporium and creative consultancy.

For £35 you could have a one person, 3,200 cubic feet capacity balloon with a circumference of 57 feet, 'as supplied to Norton and Company, Sydney [Australia]'. The price included 500 feet of rope, ballast bags, a 25 foot long, 5 inch diameter hose pipe 'to conduct gas into the balloon', a net to cover the balloon and bespoke sign-writing to go round its 'equator'. You paid £2-10s extra for a windlass to wind the balloon up and down.

If you wanted to take friends up with you, a thirty thousand cubic feet capacity balloon for three was available with all equipment for £150. You could also commission a 'War Balloon of any description, a Scientific Ascent, an ascent for your fete or gala or a juvenile balloon race' for your garden party.

It was not all plain sailing through the clouds. Balloon manufacturers, even those with the monopoly enjoyed at first by the Spencers, needed to enhance their income by all possible means. So almost as soon as the first aeronauts floated up into the skies, they began encouraging people to pay for leaflets to be dropped on the population below. Spencers developed 'Advertising by Balloon' to a considerable pitch by around 1888. 'We would point out that publicity may be given to a whole Town at one time by a Captive Balloon with large block letters painted round the equator, with the announcements. These balloons are let up several hundred feet, and at night illuminated by Incandescent Electric Lights. Thousands of small handbills may be liberated from the balloon.'

Mr Percival Spencer

Capⁿ Arthur Spencer

Capⁿ Stanley Spencer

fig. 33–35. Percival, Arthur and Stanley: the Spencer Brothers aeronauts

For the go-ahead advertiser, captive balloons, like those of today, could be provided in all sorts of shapes and sizes. Messrs John Gosnell bought one in the shape of their 'Cherry Blossom Perfume' bottle; Messrs Barrett had one in the shape of their 'Screw Stoppered Stout and Ale Bottle'.

You could also buy little balloons, put advertising slogans or anything else on them and let them go with the wind. 'Ten thousand inflated by us in Hyde Park on the occasion of the Children's Jubilee Fete, June 22 1887.' For parties 17 shillings and sixpence would buy you a 'Goldbeaters skin animal balloon' in the shape of a salamander, a sea monster or a swallow. And the balloon lover who had everything could splash out £3-10s on an enormous inflatable horse and jockey.

A new opportunity floated Spencers' way with the development of the parachute. Parachutes were of rigid design, like Cocking's, until 1885 when an American called van Tassel invented a mushroom-shaped version that drooped unopened from the bottom of a balloon basket until the parachutist jumped. Then their weight dragged on a line attached to the parachute and forced air into the canopy.

Thomas Scott Baldwin, a wire-walker, first demonstrated this type of parachute in Golden Gate Park, San Francisco, on the 30 January 1885. He astonished a crowd of 30,000 people with a successful jump from a tethered balloon.

Van Tassel and Baldwin then had an argument over the sharing of profits from the parachuting. Baldwin broke the partnership, secured a patent for a parachute not unlike van Tassel's design, and headed for England. By the time he reached Alexandra Palace in 1888 he had promoted himself to 'Professor' or 'Captain' Baldwin. Despite venomous attacks from peers of the realm and newspaper editorials, Professor Baldwin gave an immensely successful series of demonstrations at the Ally Pally. Then he was off again to Australia on his world tour and a career that took him way beyond parachuting and eventually to fame as the 'father of American aviation'.

Percy rushed into his own parachute jumping career and developed teams of aeronauts to capitalise on the new sensation. All this activity brought him to the notice of such celebrities as James Glaisher and Major Baden Baden Powell, brother of BP of scouting fame; they were members of the Balloon Society's committee that elected him as the Society's official aeronaut on 12th December 1888 .

By then the firm was CG Spencer and Sons: Arthur and Stanley, Percy's brothers, had joined him. A second company, Spencer Brothers Aeronauts, was created to supply pilots for displays or private ascents. The name of the firm was somewhat unfair on Julia Spencer, who was heavily involved in the early days touring galas, Bank Holiday shows and all sorts of other public events.

An Indian entrepreneur saw one of Percy's early jumps and invited him to Bombay (now Mumbai). He accepted immediately, set off in 1889 and made the first ever parachute jump in India above the grounds of Government House, Parel, which had been the official summer residence of the governors of Bombay.

Bombay offered a good supply of the Spencers' normal balloon 'fuel', coal gas. Calcutta (Kolkata), the next stop, was not so conveniently equipped. The racecourse where the balloon was to take off, was a long way from the gas works; the coal gas quality was so poor that it could not be used. Hydrogen was available but the supply was slow and inflation was taking an age. Percy was keen not to disappoint the large crowd (he claimed it numbered 250,000) and was, possibly, alarmed by their attitude: they were 'becoming impatient', according to one account. The presence of the Viceroy, Lord Lansdowne, and many maharajahs and other notables, may have also have encouraged recklessness.

PERCIVAL SPENCER'S ASCENT
AT CALCUTTA.

fig. 36. Percy's balloon at Calcutta: the slow inflation

For whatever reason, Percy took a risk that nearly killed him. He gave up the idea of a parachute jump and took off without basket, ballast, grapnel and gas release valve. Sitting on a simple sling below the half inflated balloon, he sailed off over the heads of the crowd. John Bacon describes the situation. '…the short tropical twilight soon gave way to darkness, when the intrepid voyager disappeared completely from sight. Excitement was intense that night in Calcutta, and greater still the next day when, as hour after hour went by, no news save a series of wild and false reports reached the city…The Great Eastern Hotel, where the young man had been staying, was literally besieged for hours by a large crowd eager for any tidings… From the direction the balloon had taken, it was thought that even if the aeronaut had descended in safety, he could only have been landed in the jungle of the Sunderbunds, beset with perils, and without a chance of succour.' *The Indian Mirror* of March 22nd 1889 headlined its story 'The tragic end of Mr. Percival Spencer' and spoke of the aeronaut's 'terrible doom.' This became one of Percy's most prized press cuttings.

Three days later he was back in Calcutta. He had been astonishingly lucky. The balloon climbed very high and took him 36 miles south-west. It then descended in the darkness, more or less where the locals had feared it might, among the creeks and crocodiles of the Ganges Delta nearest the sea. The area, now the Sunderban National Park, is a mangrove eco-system that is home to the largest remaining population of Bengal tigers.

Percy did not land in a creek or on an alligator or in the mouth of a Bengal tiger. He jumped to safety as the balloon lost sufficient hydrogen and lift to carry him and touched down on a spit of land. Freed of his weight, the balloon instantly disappeared towards the sea.

After a long walk round one creek after another, Percy saw a light shining from a small group of buildings and made his way towards them. The family who lived there saw him coming and were terrified by the appearance of a bearded white stranger advancing on them in the middle of the night on the furthest reaches of the Delta, apparently without transport. Percy persuaded them of his good intentions by drawing pictures of his flight and distributing some cash presents.

After that things kept getting better. Percy was given rice and goat's milk and allowed to sleep for the night on the veranda. He only learnt next day by sign conversations of his good fortune in landing in a clearing and avoiding the deep woods and crocodile-infested creeks.

A boat was found to take Percy back up the river to Calcutta. Just after starting the return journey, he saw that the tide had brought in his balloon, which had not, after all, gone far out to sea. He packed it up again and continued his journey.

If his departure had been heroic, his return was simply magnificent, reminiscent of the arrival of a viceroy rather than of a North London balloon maker. Bacon tells us, 'The greeting was enthusiastic beyond description from both Europeans and natives. The hero of the adventure was visited by rajahs and notables, who vied with each other in expressions of welcome, in making presents, even inviting him to visit the sacred precincts of their zenanas.'

We do not know what Percy made of the zenanas, or harems, and still less what the massed wives of the rajahs made of him. But he had no time for extended socialising: he had a living to earn. He changed his launch site to the yard of the Calcutta coal gas works at Narkeldanga, made an ally of the works manager, and began a series of flights that included parachute jumps and a scientific ascent for the Meteorological Department of India.

He met the Tsarevich (Crown Prince) of Russia in Madras. This was five years before the Tsarevich's succession to the throne as Nicholas II after his father's assassination and 19 years before his own death at the hands of the Bolsheviks. Nicholas gave Percy Spencer a jewelled scarf-pin, which he wore at every opportunity for the rest of his life.

On the 10th April 1889, Spencer took up a pupil, Ramchunder Chatterjee, who had paid him five hundred rupees to learn ballooning. Ramchunder was an expert trapeze artist in the Indian National Circus Company and, in the tradition of that company, sought to provide a nationally bred alternative to the visits of European showmen . He was heralded as the first Indian aeronaut and by the 4th May 1889 had bought Percy's balloon 'Viceroy of India', renamed it 'City of Calcutta' and flown it for forty minutes in his first solo flight.

Percy was meanwhile off back to England for his summer bookings and a visit to Dublin in September, where he made the first parachute jump recorded in Ireland. But his world travel was not over. He soon sailed away again on the long sea passage through the Suez Canal and was back in Bombay by November 1889. This tour took him back to Calcutta for a brief season of display jumps, and then a little further up the Ganges to Allahabad. Percy did not risk doubtful supplies of gas on his second Indian trip. He brought one of Spencers' little asbestos fire (hot air) balloons with him so that, regardless of the quality of the coal gas supply, he could ascend and parachute wherever his assistants had space to build a fire pit and fuel to burn.

He resumed his tuition of Ramchunder and supervised the Indian's first, triumphantly successful, parachute jump above Calcutta's Tivoli Gardens on the 22nd March. Percy gave him a specially cast medal to commemorate the feat. Ramchunder's jump and his balloon ascent was significant under the colonial conditions in India. It was 'an extension of the patriotic gesture... an effort to come to terms with the Europeans at their own game.' Sadly, Ramchunder died of terrible injuries after a jumping accident in April 1892. But his short

fig. 37. Charles Green Spencer's monument in Highgate Cemetery

career and Percival Spencer's support had opened a path for other Indian aeronauts. These included Ramchunder's daughter, who probably made parachute descents herself.

Back in England the Spencer family scene was changing. First, on the 17th February 1890, Percy's uncle Edward, the post office clerk and family archivist, died. Edward was the oldest of the brothers and was close to George Spencer rather than Charles and Percy, so the news may not have been very distressing. But news soon to come would change Percy's life dramatically.

He headed east from India to a booking in Singapore. For this jump, he wore a cork jacket in case he found himself parachuting into the sea. But the jacket was not necessary. All went without a hitch.

Percy did get wet when he moved on to Japan. On an ascent at Kobe, he miscalculated the wind's speed and direction, landed in the sea and had to be pulled out by the crew of a passing fishing boat. In Tokyo the Mikado watched another performance that went rather better. Percy rose serenely from the palace grounds below his balloon, jumped at 5,000 feet and parachuted gently and accurately to a landing within a few metres (25 feet) of the richly decorated tent of the Mikado and his Empress. The Mikado was impressed and offered a choice of rewards: a piece of Imperial furniture, a Japanese honour or coin of the realm. Percy took the coin of the realm.

Next stop was Sumatra, then part of the Dutch East Indies, where the Dutch were fighting the Achinese War, a long and bloody colonial conflict. The Dutch generals became interested in Percy's balloon as an observation platform. *The Times*, which normally took a snooty and disinterested position on ballooning, published a 'Letter about the experiment of using the war balloon in the Dutch war' from one of their correspondents.

The letter reported that the Dutch were sending 'a military ballooning contingent under the direction of Mr Percival Spencer, an English aeronaut, to Kota Rajah, the fortified capital of the unconquered regions, where it is proposed to establish a permanent balloon reconnoitering corps to watch, and if possible circumvent the strategical movements of the enemy. The gas used for inflation is apparently 'powered by a portable apparatus made of his own invention…'

The Dutch army tethered Percy and his balloon to a long rope high above the back of an armoured train and set off towards the enemy. The rebels correctly decided that the sudden appearance of a balloon meant them no good and opened fire on Percy and the officer he had taken up in the basket with him. But their shots went wide and Percy returned unscathed. We do not know if anything further was heard of 'the balloon reconnoitering corps'.

After all these adventures it was time for Percy to set off for England. He did not hurry back, however and stopped off in Egypt for long enough to make a parachute jump by the Pyramids before heading for home.

His status had changed dramatically while he had been away. Charles Green Spencer, his father, had died on the 4th June 1890 and Percy was now head of the firm. The family buried Charles' ashes in Highgate Cemetery. His cremation was one of the first permitted in England and his grave was marked with a monument that carried a fine balloon in relief.

fig. 38. Percy's family at tea. Left to right: Baby Hilda , a visitor, Dorothy, Marie, Mary Spencer (nee Coleman), Charles. The photograph probably dates from late 1899/early 1900. Courtesy of Ruth Fryer

VII

Sister & brother aeronauts

Percy now toured less, but the other Spencer brothers continued sailing the seas with balloons and parachutes packed in the ships' holds. Foreign touring extended the season splendidly.

Julia, their sister, never toured abroad, but may well have been the first English woman parachutist. According to Dolly Shepherd, a highly successful parachutist in the 1900s, the late Victorian/Edwardian barnstorming parachuting teams always included women, usually dressed in knickerbocker suits or something equally daring. Dolly's daughter, Molly Sedgwick, told me that only two things were necessary for a woman to be taken on as a parachutist: good looks and a strong grip.

Stanley Spencer went to South Africa. He was not the first balloonist there. 'In the 1890s many showmen balloonists performed throughout the country with their hot air bags and parachutes. The first and most successful of these was an American, Professor James William Price, who over a 10-year period made some 100 flights, and also managed more than a dozen pilots, both male and female. …in January 1892 the well known balloonist from England, Mr. Stanley Spencer toured the country giving demonstrations and lectures.'

Arthur contributed an expedition to Australia with two balloons, one of which could hold 80,000 cubic feet of gas. British sailors were borrowed to help with an inflation for an ascent from Melbourne Exhibition Ground on Boxing Day, 1897. They started funnelling in gas at 10am on Christmas Day, continued to six o'clock when the balloon was half-full, and went off to their Christmas dinner. Inflation began again at 4am on Boxing Day and went well under a cloudless sky. But at around 6.30 pm a terrific squall blew up.

On the windward side of the balloon, twelve men, despite the weight of 220 sandbags, were lifted straight up into the air. Mercifully the silk envelope of the balloon, which was almost fully inflated, slid out of the netting that held it. The sailors were dropped to the ground without serious injuries. The envelope eventually crashed ninety miles away and was a total write-off.

fig. 39. The Reverend John Bacon ready to receive aerial messages

AFTER THE "LEONID" VOYAGE

fig. 40. John Bacon and his daughter Gertrude after trying to see the Leonids

Stanley was meanwhile getting noticed nearer home. The Spencers liked the scientific aspects of ballooning, particularly if it involved paying customers. The 1890s and early 1900s experiments often involved the Bacon family. In 1899, astronomers were predicting the spectacular return of the Leonids, the meteor shower. So, at 4am on the 16th November, John Bacon and his daughter, Gertrude , with Stanley Spencer as pilot, took off from Newbury Gas Works in fine drizzle. Hundreds had turned out to see them rise into the darkness until out of sight in thick cloud 1500 feet high. The balloon made slow progress upwards, despite bag after bag of sand ballast being emptied over the side.

Then, one more sandbag was discharged and 'the vapour broke above our heads and we emerged into a realm of beauty aloft that none but we three in all the world were privileged to enter… For us a full moon reigned glorious in the heaven. For us alone Sirius flashed magnesium blue, and the other stars glistened as jewels in a blue black velvet sky. We had scarcely room for disappointment that the marvellous shower had never come after all.'

They soon forgot meteor hunting: the balloon was sinking back into the mist as the silk envelope was saturated with moisture. Bacon brushed aside Stanley Spencer's proposal that they should allow themselves to drift down the the ground and insisted they should throw out more precious sand. They rose above the mist and ate sandwiches while listening to the early rumbles of trains on the Great Western Railway and 'the rhythmic clatter' of horses' hooves on the Bath Road. It began to grow light. But the beauty of the dawn did not bring peace of mind. They were caught in a trap, as Stanley had almost certainly feared.

As the sun warmed the balloon, the gas expanded and took them higher and higher. Only after noon could they hope that cooling, and descent, would begin. They did not mind the extra time in the balloon basket, though cramped and eating sand with the sandwiches. They were more worried that they were heading towards the Atlantic Ocean. The thick cloud obscured what was below. 'All too soon, arose the shrill well-remembered shriek of a ship's steam siren, and mingled with it was the clash and clang of hammers in the dockyard seaport town. But more ominous far than these was that gentle rhythmic beat… the sound of breaking waves upon a pebbly beach.'

Above the clouds the sun was uncomfortably hot. Bacon had dropped his cap earlier in the voyage and improvised a head covering from a handkerchief knotted at the corners as if he was on Blackpool beach. 'The knotted ends… hung in ridiculous fashion about his grey whiskers and patriarchal beard.'

They had no idea where they were but could hear the sea beneath them. Occasional sounds, which might have come from a seaport, still came up to the balloon. Bacon organised his younger companions into drafting a press telegram for *The Times*, photographing the clouds that stretched as far as they could see and writing and dropping dozens of notes warning of their plight which they hoped someone would take to the Coast Guard.

At last it was noon. Almost immediately, Bacon, who was watching the barometer they used to calculate their altitude, announced that they had dropped from 9000 to 7000 feet and were still going down. They were by now convinced that when they broke through the cloud they would see little but miles of Atlantic Ocean. Spencer suddenly exclaimed, 'I can see a church'. John Bacon put a hand on his shoulder and said, 'Where my good fellow? Where?'

Gertrude wrote, 'I knew that he thought the long strain and hot sun had affected our aeronaut's head.' But as they dropped further they could see that it really was a church. They had been extraordinarily fortunate and had been travelling along the Bristol Channel; they were not at sea.

But the danger was not over. Two more hours' descent brought them near the ground where a fierce gale greeted them and hurled the balloon and its basket down with a crash

fig. 41. Arthur Spencer, happy and horizontal. Courtesy the Spencer family

that broke Gertrude's right arm. Then it carried them 'in maddest steeplechase' through a barbed wire fence that ripped open John Bacon's leg. Finally they struck an oak tree, broke through all its top branches and found themselves in the overturned basket in a field beyond. Fortunately, the balloon's grapnel, which had trailed uselessly behind them in their mad career, wedged itself in the roots of the oak, and brought them to a stop. After ten hours flight, they were a mile and a half from the Atlantic and five minutes away from crash landing in a very rough sea.

John and Gertrude Bacon, battered, bandaged and plastered with mud, presented themselves at *The Times* offices in Printing House Square and handed in their copy. 'Out in the street our exploit was already on posters and headlines, passers-by identified us, policemen grinned recognition. For days the papers were full of the adventure…' Stanley may have reflected that if John Bacon had allowed his pilot to bring the balloon down before dawn, the risks of the morning flight could have been avoided. But a paying customer is a paying customer.

On a happier assignment Stanley took off from the Cork Corn Exchange during the Easter Monday Cork Park race meeting in 1901. The local paper enthused, '…the aeronaut and balloon shot into the air with the rapidity of a cannon ball, Captain Spencer waving his cap to the multitude from an altitude of 7,000 feet. At this height the parachute was detached, and the aeronaut gracefully alighted in the centre of Cork Park.'

The reporter interviewed 'Captain Spencer, who is an extremely courteous and cultured gentleman'. Stanley told him that he and his brothers had travelled 'the whole world including Europe, Asia, Africa and America. At this point, the aeronaut pointed with a sense of much delight to two handsome gold medals he was wearing. The first medal was

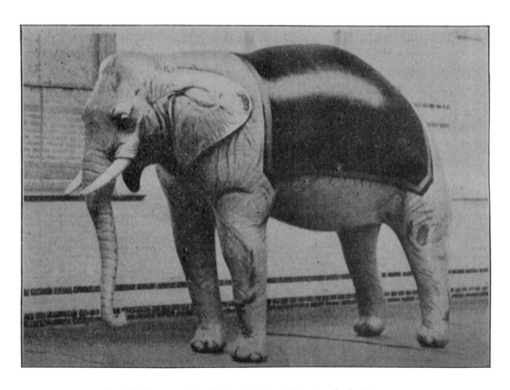

fig. 42. You want a flying elephant? Just ask the Spencers

presented to him on the 18 February '93, in recognition of his being the first parachutist to appear on the isle of Cuba. The second medal was presented for the highest ascent on record, which was performed on the 15th September, '98, from the Crystal Palace Grounds, London. The altitude reached by Capt. Spencer on that occasion was 27,000 feet. He was accompanied by the celebrated Dr Berson on that ascent.'

Berson was a pioneering meteorologist, based in Berlin, who understood the possibilities of high altitude aeronautics. He had already made an extraordinary 30,000 feet solo ascent from Berlin on September/December 4th, 1894 in the *Phoenix*, a 92,000 cubic feet balloon, in which he travelled up to 30,000 feet.

The aeronauts had prepared carefully for the ascent. Stanley explained that they travelled up in a clear blue sky to 23,000 feet before being hit by lack of oxygen. They then inhaled oxygen through tubes. '…new life seemed to come into us and we were enabled to continue the reading of our instruments, of which we had many of various kinds. We then continued our journey to a higher point when the atmosphere fell to 61 degrees below zero. Every hook on the balloon's pegs and every piece of metal, including some of the instruments were covered in ice.'

They reached 27,000 feet but then decided they had to come down, because the long ascent had used all but four of their sandbags. They let out a little gas and began their descent. At 20,000 feet, they could see the coast of France though they were still directly over London. Then things got tricky. 'We threw out two of the remaining four bags of sand we had, and so rapid was the descent that the sand, instead of falling, shot into the air like a cloud. We then threw out our last two bags of sand. This somewhat checked our rapid descent, but we were soon startled on hearing a sound similar to that of hailstones. This noise proved to be that the

*fig. 43. The Graphic balloon carried Percy and John Bacon on many adventures.
The 'petals' round the base of the gasbag are a Spencer trademark. Courtesy the Spencer family*

sand, which we had thrown out on the first occasion, was catching us up and rattling up.' But all eventually ended happily: the aeronauts came down into 'a more dense atmosphere', and a relatively gentle landing near Romford in Kent.

Berson was to go higher still. Four months after Stanley gave that interview in Cork, Berson surpassed the two person and every other altitude record. He and his Berlin colleagues had learnt from his earlier flights and built a balloon named *Preussen* (German for Prussia) which used 300,000 cubic feet of gas to fill its gigantic envelope. Berson and a Dr Suring went up to 35,000 feet in this monster on 31st July,1901.

L.T.C Rolt notes that this record for manned ascent was not surpassed until Piccard began high altitude flights using a pressurised gondola in 1931. Berson and other meteorologists knew they were taking greater and greater risks as they soared higher and higher with the equipment of the 1900s and moved, sensibly, to the use of unmanned balloons for high altitude investigations.

Meanwhile the Spencers continued their international tours. Stanley claimed to have been the victim of a bizarre accident in Hong Kong. While his balloon was being inflated one of the thirty men holding it down cut the envelope with his exceptionally long fingernails. 'An immense rent three yards square' appeared in the balloon but Stanley thought he could get away with an ascent. 'The balloon was let loose with myself hanging beneath it [on the sling from which he was intending to parachute]. But he was out of luck. The balloon only carried him up to 600 feet. 'The balloon rolled from top to bottom. Down I came and I tried desperately to wrench the parachute from the balloon. In this I failed and I descended like an arrow until I reached some steep sloping cliffs on the water's edge. I struck the slope of the cliff down the side of which I slided (sic) until the speed of the descent was checked by some stubbley bush. This contact made me spin round. And in making an attempt to get up I found to my grief and horror that I had broken my leg.' Stanley lay where he was until picked up and taken to hospital by some British sailors whose battleship was stationed at Hong Kong. He had to stay in hospital for six weeks and was lucky to be left with only the slightest of limps.

Percy was often consulted on aeronautical matters. In 1897 the Swedish explorer Andree proposed to fly a balloon to the North Pole. He came to London and sought out Percy to discuss his idea. He thought he could steer his balloon to the Pole by use of a drag rope and sail. Percy knew all about drag ropes. Charles Green, his grandfather's friend, had invented the technique as a means of stabilizing a balloon's height without the use of ballast. Percy worked out that the technique proposed would only allow the Arctic aeronauts to veer the course of their balloon by a few degrees. Worse than that, the plan to steer a free balloon over a planned route through the unpredictable winds of the Arctic was foolhardy to say the least.

Percy sensibly recommended a delay and some trial flights over the fringe of the icesheet. Andree did not heed Percy's or anyone else's warnings. He took off with two companions in a new, untested balloon, laden with equipment and supplies, to fly to the Pole on July 11th 1897. Sure enough, a ship's captain in the area reported that the winds over the next week veered widely all the way from south west to north west.

We know that the aeronauts stayed up in the air for at least two days because a week or so after the ascent, Norwegian fishermen shot a pigeon with a note from the balloonists attached to its leg. The note was dated 13th July and read 'All goes well'. Andree and his party were not heard of again.

The mystery of their fate was solved 33 years later when three bodies, together with diaries and photographs, were found at a camp on the ice. Loss of gas had forced the aeronauts down shortly after the cheerful pigeon post of the 13th July. All three survived for several

fig. 44. Aerial view of the York Gala, about 1902

fig. 45. A horse and cart provided the transport at the end of most balloon adventures.
Courtesy the Spencer family

months, trekking and trekking across shifting ice but unable to reach safety. Eventually they made a camp in which to see out the winter. But they were weakened by their ordeal and died sometime in October 1897.

Arthur Spencer was unfortunate on one of the firm's Bank Holiday bookings. He was due to jump at Pontypool in Wales on the afternoon of Easter Monday, 8th April 1901, when a terrific hail and rainstorm broke over the Recreation Grounds. This lasted half an hour and delayed thoughts of a launch for considerably longer, as Arthur was using a hot air balloon. His team got the balloon inflated just before 5pm. According to the *Pontypool Free Press*, 'up went the balloon bearing the intrepid captain with a bound, followed by the shouts of thousands of admiring spectators.' The balloon rose to about 4000 feet but was still very damp and could go no higher. Arthur decided to jump. The parachute opened perfectly and Arthur looked set for a good landing in a field by nearby Trevethin Church. But, when he was almost down, a cross current blew him straight across to the churchyard. 'After barely clearing a yew tree the parachute suddenly collapsed', as it blew into the lee of the church. 'Captain Spencer dropped heavily, and was driven against a tombstone with such force as to displace the cross which formed the top. He was then carried on to the top of a higher tombstone standing about 12 feet away, and fell to the ground close to some spiked railings.' Arthur was conscious but seriously injured, though matters could have been worse if he had dropped on to the spiked railings.

He was swiftly 'taken to the Yew Tree Inn where he had every consideration given to him by Mr and Mrs Price, the landlord and landlady, and Miss Carrick, the district nurse.' A doctor arrived and decided that Arthur's most serious problem was a fractured left thigh. Percy, who had had a difficult landing that Monday at Crystal Palace, rushed down by train to bring his brother back to London. By Thursday Arthur was in St Mary's Hospital, Paddington. He made a good recovery, but rarely jumped again. He became the full time factory manager and was fit enough to take over Spencer Brothers as managing director after Percy's death.

Press cuttings covering C.G. Spencer and Sons' ballooning and parachuting between 1901 and 1906 have survived. They provide an almost complete account of everything the firm did during those years, including records of accidents and injuries. So we know that the serious accident to Arthur Spencer was unusual and that members of Spencers' teams rarely suffered major injury before the First World War.

In contrast, as Dolly Shepherd makes clear, the Gaudron teams often suffered accidents during the same period. The difference between the teams may reflect on Gaudron's management, but is more likely to relate to the fact that he was working within tighter financial margins than Percy Spencer. The manager of a firm with few financial reserves was more likely to demand that a parachutist went up (and down) in risky circumstances than one who could afford to cancel a performance in poor conditions. Similarly, teams with lower budgets could be at risk from poorly maintained equipment. As we shall see, the accidents to Spencers' teams after 1918 may well have related to the tough financial climate in which they were operating.

fig. 46. One of the four balloons used in the 1901 Hudsons Soap roadshow. Courtesy the Spencer family

VIII

The best of times

This story began in the coronation year of Queen Victoria. By Edward VII's coronation in 1902, Spencers' balloon and parachute enterprises were at the height of their popularity. Percy, Stanley and the others were famous across the land and round the world.

Earnings were steady, even if profits were not spectacular. The teams were indispensable at fetes, galas and private balloon races. Advertising by balloon was reaching new heights. In 1901 Percy arranged Spencers' biggest ever roadshow: captive ascents of four balloons at a time took the Hudsons Soap brand in letters two metres high across England, Ireland, Scotland and Wales. The Peek Frean biscuits marketing team printed half a million tickets and Spencers threw them out all over London. The person who collected the most tickets could claim £25.

Gugliemo Marconi took some small Spencer balloons and Baden Baden-Powell kites to Newfoundland to test his system of transatlantic wireless communication. The kites and balloons were to take an aerial high into the air to catch Morse Code tapped out at the Poldhu transmitter station, 2100 miles away on the Lizard in Cornwall. Newfoundland gales carried away one balloon and two kites. But, on the 12th December 1901, a kite-flown aerial stayed in place and picked up the signal, a success for Baden Powell, and a triumph for Marconi.

Spencers' factory was busy, particularly in the summer season. Percy explained the trades involved in building a balloon to the *Manchester Evening Chronicle* in 1904. 'The silk weaver for the gas-vessel, the ironmonger for the anchor, the ropemaker for the net, the basket-maker for the car, the carpenter for the wood-work, the sailor for the knotting and splicing, the paint and varnish maker, the scientific instrument maker, and the sewing machine workers'.

Living London, published in 1901, gave more detail. 'Here… many balloons in all stages may be seen in progress of manufacture, and at first sight it seems surprising on entering that so much and varied work can proceed within confusion within so limited an area.

IN A BALLOON FACTORY.

fig. 47. Inside Spencers' factory. Photograph by John Bacon

But a glance at the workmen themselves suffices to dispel the mystery. With many of them the weather-beaten face, the easy attitude, the deftly working fingers, at once betray the old sailor…

Spread out over nearly half the available floor space lies a balloon lately come home from active service, which is being overhauled and examined in every detail, or if necessary inflated with a rotary fan for better inspection. Hard by another balloon is receiving its coats of varnish. On a long side table the gores of a new balloon are being cut out with the sweep of a razor, while upstairs women are sewing the huge lengths together. Hanging from a line across the far corner a net of gigantic mesh, worked by hand, is assuming large proportions; while elsewhere carpenters are at work upon wooden valves, and cars [baskets], with their appropriate hoops, are being fitted and rigged.'

So the manufacturing techniques of the sailing ship and the fishing port were the foundation of the Spencers' enterprise as they entered the twentieth century. Grandfather Edward's notes on balloon-building provided the basis of the technology.

Percy always found time to sit in his study in Aberdeen Park, Islington, to stick press cuttings on aeronautics and Spencer exploits into a large brown album. One 1904 page shows Stanley showering cheques onto London passers-by in a stunt for a new daily paper; the next records the completion of the Wright Brothers' latest experiments with their new heavier-than-air flying machine.

Once the cuttings were stuck down, Percy could check the neatness of his beard, adjust the scarf-pin given him by Tsar Nicholas II and stroll across his back garden to monitor progress on current projects in the factory.

Stanley Spencer and his wife Rose lived next door to Percy and Mary. There could be tension between the households. Rose made a small rockery outside the front of their house. Percy kicked it down one morning. He apologised most politely, according to Ena, Auguste and Marina Gaudron's daughter, 'I am sorry, Rose. My bowels hadn't moved.'

But Percy was well loved. Charles, his son, remembered him lying on the floor after Sunday lunch with his two little daughters, Hilda and Violet, sitting on his tummy as he smoked a cigar .

At that time Spencers only had two British competitors. As we have seen, the first was almost part of the family. Up the road from their Islington headquarters, their ex-apprentice, Auguste Gaudron, had his base at Alexandra Palace. Gaudron came to London after training at the Lachambre balloon factory in Paris. He married Marina Spencer, and became a close working partner of Henry (Harry) Spencer, the fourth of the brothers. Marina helped Auguste establish his parachute team and sometimes jumped herself; they travelled together to France and Russia.

The teams sometimes shared staff. For example, Viola Kavanagh, who may have been a cousin, jumped for both Spencers and Gaudron's teams.

Though the Spencers were generally fortunate in their ascents and parachute jumps, performances in Wales were particularly accident-prone. Stanley offered captive ascents in his balloon *Excellent* at the Cardiff Horticultural Society's 1894 show and the show committee went up for a ride. They were on their way down when the winch reeling them back to earth jammed. A strong wind blew the balloon against a tree. Some committee members jumped out onto it and clambered down to earth. The Chairman had to cling desperately to a branch before being rescued. Fortunately there were no injuries and the crowd found the chaotic descent better entertainment than the ascent.

After that near-disaster, the committee for the 1896 Cardiff Fine Art, Industrial and Maritime Exhibition avoided Spencer Brothers and booked Auguste Gaudron for balloon and parachute displays in Cathay Park. For one parachute show, Gaudron announced a performance by 'the celebrated parachutist, Mademoiselle Albertina'.

'Looking young and diminutive with refined features and girlish blue eyes,' she waved to the huge crowd as she went up. '…up to an unprecedented 6,000 feet [1830 metres], then the drop. But the cheers were silenced as her parachute drifted away, the balloon coming down off the mouth of the Rhymney River. But no Mademoiselle Albertina. Her body was found three days later on the riverbank near Newport. It turned out that far from being Mademoiselle Albertina, renowned parachutist, she was Louisa Maude Evans, only 14 years old, making her first parachute drop after persuading Professor Gaudron she was experienced.'

The inquest jury foreman addressed the court. 'Our unanimous verdict is, that the deceased was accidentally drowned in the Bristol Channel whilst attempting to descend by parachute from a balloon… We wish to censor Mr Gaudron, showman and balloon aeronaut, in that he showed great carelessness and disregard for the safety of such a young girl by allowing her to attempt her descent during such high winds. '

Louisa Maud was buried in Cardiff on July 29, her memorial stone purchased by public subscription.

No other British firm showed interest in the parachute jumping market at that date, but in 1901 the brothers Eustace and Oswald Short became balloon-makers. Their first flights took place in a secondhand Spencer balloon, the *Queen of the West*. Oswald Short wrote: 'It

fig. 48. The inaugural ascent of the newly formed Aero Club. 'The City of York' about to start

was very old and rattled as we filled it… It was blown and worn, so as we filled it we had to have sticking plaster put on.' Shorts then built their own balloon, and named it, reasonably enough, *New Balloon*. By 1902, according to their records, they had only made eleven ascents. The Spencers and Auguste Gaudron will not have been worried.

While more and more people were refusing to tolerate the inequalities of English society, the world of the rich was largely unaffected. They could afford ballooning. For twenty pounds or so you could hire a pilot to take you up from Hurlingham with friends, a picnic and a bottle or two of champagne. When you came home, you could collapse into a hot bath and read the latest instalment of Conan Doyle's *Hound of the Baskervilles* in the *Strand Magazine*. Or if, as Harry Harper recounts, you only arrived in London in time for a late dinner, you could take a hansom-cab down Piccadilly or the Strand and spend 'the rest of the evening in one or other of London's old music-halls, joining lustily in the chorus of whatever song might be the hit of the moment.'

The Spencers were well positioned to take advantage of the interest in aeronautics. On the 24th September 1901, Stanley Spencer was piloting the *City of York* balloon high above South London. He was with Frank Hedges-Butler, aviation enthusiast and wine merchant to King Edward VII, Vera, his daughter, and C.S. 'Charlie' Rolls, who had not yet met Royce, but was already mad about motor cars: he was known as 'Dirty Rolls' at Eton because of his coatings in oil. The young Spencers knew him, less affectionately, as 'old Popeyes'. Ena suggests that the two Short Brothers were working for Spencers when Rolls 'stole' them to start a rival aeronautics business. I have found no evidence of this, but Ena, as an only child, certainly heard the gossip. She writes knowingly about Rolls' lady friend Hon Mrs Assheton Harbord: 'quite a story that, this little pitcher had big ears, perhaps being an 'only one' with no playmates, heard more than you.'

The Hedges-Butlers had planned to start a motoring holiday that day. But Vera's car was damaged, so they opted for a consolation balloon flight from Crystal Palace, the Spencers' south London base, and invited Rolls to join them. Once high in the air, conversation turned to the support that the Aeroclub de France was giving aeronautics in Paris. The legend says that Vera took her companions the short step to the proposal that they should found an Aero Club of the United Kingdom. By the time they landed the club was established.

Harry Harper claims that the formation of the Aero Club 'turned ballooning from a showman's game to a fashionable sport'. Less than a dozen balloons were in private ownership in the early 1900s; many more were needed for the massed ascents from Hurlingham and Ranelagh club grounds in the summer. So the rental market grew rapidly and the distinctive flared emblems at the base of Spencer balloon envelopes appeared regularly in press photographs of the events.

Spencers' *City of York* balloon was chosen for the first official Aero Club ascent, at Stamford Bridge in West London on the 15th November,1901. The three founding members were there with Stanley Spencer and a new, heavy Aero Club flag. The balloon could not lift four people and the flag. Rolls jumped out with the cry 'I will sacrifice myself for the flag.' The incident did not damage relations with the Club: the Spencers went on to build the *Aeroclub No. 1*, its first balloon. Rolls gave £10 towards the cost.

While trips in lighter-than-air craft were now fashionable, far-sighted individuals expressed doubts about the role of the balloon or airship in the future of aviation. Hiram Maxim wrote the introduction to Valentine and Thompson's *Travels in Space* in 1902. 'In all Nature, we do not find a single balloon. All Nature's flying machines are heavier than the air, and depend altogether on the development of dynamic energy. In Nature's machines the amount of energy developed for a given weight is very great indeed, but no greater than the artificial motors which we have been able to produce at the present time. It is quite true that a bird can develop a great deal more energy for a pound of carbon consumed than it is possible to develop with any artificial motor, but on the other hand, Nature has not yet developed a bird that can feed on petroleum, and petroleum carries much more energy in proportion to its weight than any food on which it is possible for a bird to feed.'

Maxim knew where answers to the problems of heavier-than-air flight would be found. 'in England, France and the United States there has been fully a million pounds sterling spent in the last six years on experiments connected with the development of gasoline motors for motor-cars, and this development is always in the direction of efficiency and lightness... Then again, the motor-car industry has done much towards providing suitable materials such as strong steel tubes and wires, and light and strong aluminium castings, thus furnishing the flying machine experimenter with the exact material he requires without having to pay for the experiments himself.' Percy accepted that a heavier-than-air machine would fly sometime '...the theory of the thing is correct', but argued, 'In the meanwhile do not let us discard the balloon which has already been brought to such a state of perfection.' (*Church Family Newspaper* 25.1.01)

With a few exceptions, such as its support for the tiny Farnborough balloon factory, the British government ignored the possibilities of civil and military aviation throughout the early 1900s. Harry Harper describes the attitude:

'...our War Office chiefs looked upon military operations as a sort of game, a game to be played to a set of rules which on no account must be altered... as they had spent a lot of time and trouble learning those particular rules, they were not going to let anybody come along with any newfangled machine, such as the aeroplane, which might have the effect of altering and upsetting all their pet ways of playing this game...'

Charles Turner notes that the number of British aeronautical patents stayed at a low level, around an average of 30 per annum, until 1907 when 82 were registered, quickly surpassed by the 145 taken out in 1908.

Only in April 1909 could Major Squier of the US Army Signal Corps write,'each of the principal military powers is displaying feverish activity in developing this [air power] as an adjunct to the military establishment'.

Back in 1900 there was serious money across the Channel: with support from public subscription, Count Zeppelin built an enormous 'navigable balloon' at Lake Constance. Closer to home for the Spencers, financial resources were pouring into a project in Paris. This was not French government money, but money from the grano d'oro, the 'golden' coffee bean.

The Brazilian Alberto Santos-Dumont had a vast inheritance from the family coffee plantations. He spent some of this in Paris on a series of small navigable balloons; by 1901 he was trialling his fourth airship. It is arguable that the French government' s contribution to Santos-Dumont's efforts was in kind, rather than cash. French technical education was of a high standard. Experimenters also had support from the experts of the Paris balloon factories. '[Dumont] has had,' wrote Maxim,' the advantage of the experience of the French balloon-makers, who have probably reduced the balloon to as high a degree of efficiency as regards lightness and strength as it is possible to do.'

Moreover, as Rolt says, most of the technology Santos-Dumont needed was available: all that was lacking was a light, powerful engine. Santos-Dumont was a motorist, naturally, and had a petrol engine from a motor tricycle with a low weight to power ratio. 'I built an airship for my little tricycle motor', he said.

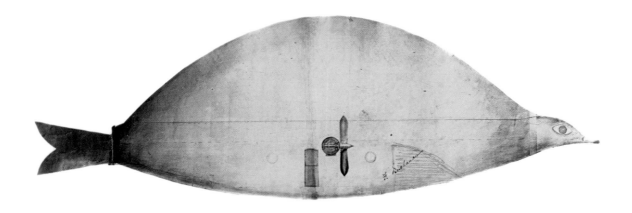

fig. 49. Thomas Buchanan's airship

By his sixth airship, Santos Dumont had moved to a twelve horse power engine. He had survived some spectacular accidents, but his craft were getting better all the time. On at least one occasion, for a bet, he parked his dirigible outside his house in the Champs Elysees.

He also enjoyed startling friends waiting at a restaurant near the Bois de Boulogne by arriving in his airship and parking it on the lawn. These were not impulse flights. Santos-Dumont always had mechanics hidden near the landing spot to rush forward and steady the keel of the machine as it touched down.

He had style as well as money.

'He never wore anything in the shape of a special flying suit when piloting his small airships. He just jumped aboard them in his ordinary clothes. And on his head, instead of anything elaborate in the way of a flying helmet, he wore a bowler hat.'

In 1900 Henry Deutsch de la Meurthe of the French Aero Club, offered 100,000 francs to any aeronaut who could take off from the Aero Club at St. Cloud, fly across Paris to the Eiffel Tower, circle it and fly back to the starting point within half an hour.

Thomas Buchanan of Portsmouth made the first English response: he ordered an airship in the shape of a gigantic bird from the Spencers. This wacky machine, allegedly the result of twenty years thought, was to have two propellers, 'the surfaces of which were roughened with minute diagonal grooves to effect a greater grip on the air.' Spencers built the airship, but a tramp, perhaps fortunately for Buchanan's health, burned his invention and its shed to ashes before its first flight.

A South African, William Beedle, also wanted a try at the prize. He commissioned Spencers to build a sausage-shaped airship with three propellers driven by a hefty twenty eight horse power engine.

It was all too late. On the 19th October 1901, Santos-Dumont in his sixth airship sailed round the Eiffel Tower and back to St. Cloud in 29 and a half minutes. He then rubbed the noses of poorer experimenters into the mud by giving all the prize money away.

Lord Northcliffe, proprietor of the *Daily Mail*, and an enthusiastic campaigner for aviation, decided to match Deutsch by putting up £5000 for the first airship to circle St Paul's Cathedral. Spencers had to have a go. They were the acknowledged leaders of ballooning in Britain and £5000 was a lot of money.

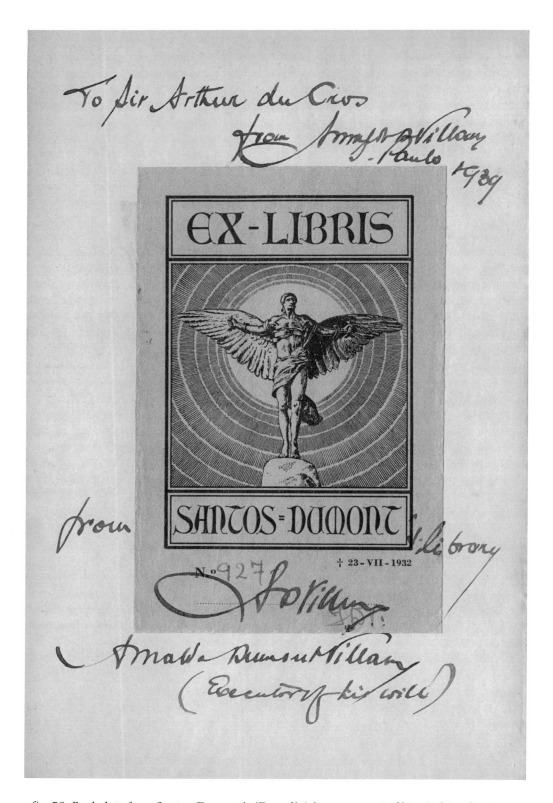

fig. 50. Bookplate from Santos-Dumont's 'Dans l'air' : an account of his airship adventures

In the meantime Santos-Dumont had been invited to England. In 1902 he sent an airship to the Crystal Palace. He was to demonstrate it and maybe, horror of horrors, undertake a flight to St Paul's Cathedral to snatch Lord Northcliffe's prize. The airship was exhibited in the Palace's concert room and then taken to a purpose-built shed for overnight storage. Two of Santos-Dumont's team were on hand to keep an eye on it. But when they unfolded the envelope of the airship the following day it was so damaged as to be unusable.

There was suspicion of sabotage. Bacon, writing soon afterwards, commented, 'In some mysterious manner, however, never sufficiently made clear to the public, this machine was one morning found damaged,' The popular press was less restrained. Under the headline 'A WANTON OUTRAGE' one paper reported

' one of the Frenchmen noticed that something was wrong [when they unfolded the envelope], and bending to examine it, exclaimed "Dechire!"(torn!). And then, growing excited, and examining deeper into the big gash, he literally gasped as he cried: "Hein! c'est fait avec des couteaux!" ("Hallo! It has been done with knives!")...while it was badly torn about the valve there were holes of various sizes all round it... That they could be accidental there is too little chance of thinking...The balloon was all right yesterday...Till eight o'clock it hung inflated in the concert room of the Palace.'

Santos-Dumont and Mr Gillman, the manager of the Crystal Palace, were horrified and called the police.

An inspector and a sergeant arrived from Gipsy Hill Police Station. Their written report to Scotland Yard has survived. The French allegations did not impress the policemen. The inspector found no sign that the envelope had been unfolded before the French team opened it. It had been locked in its shed and the workmen had been with it virtually the whole time. As clinching evidence, the police noted that they found no grit from the floor on the envelope's oiled surface, as there would have been had it been opened before the French team was there. The inspector concluded, 'I pointed all these circumstances out to Mr Gillman and M. Dumont and that everything went to show that the damage had been done by accidental causes through improper packing and not maliciously.'

But suspicions remained. Bacon was an aeronaut and a confidant of many aeronauts. Local police inspectors have sometimes been wrong or encouraged to be wrong. Crystal Palace was the Spencers' official base for flights and virtually a second home to many English balloonists. Perhaps we can allow ourselves a little caution about the authenticity of the official verdict.

Santos Dumont had no time to wait for a new envelope to be made. He had a contract to honour in New York. He left the Crystal Palace and never returned. The Northcliffe Prize was safe from foreign challenge.

fig. 51. The Spencer-Mellin airship has its first outing: 23rd June 1902

IX

The great airship adventure

The Spencers now had a clear run at the Northcliffe Prize. They were taking a great professional and financial risk. They were jobbing professional aeronauts who made balloons in a fifty year old technology. They had not benefited from a French or other extended technical education. None of them were members of the group of scientists and gentlefolk who met in the Aero Club.

On the other hand, their connections should have allowed easy access to information on building a navigable balloon. Their real problem was financial. The continental experimenters had reserves that allowed repeated experiment. The Spencers had to get things right almost first time and could do little without a sponsor.

The only sponsor to come along was a baby food manufacturer, Mellins Food. Mellins offered £1500, provided that the airship displayed Mellins Food along both sides in letters ten feet high during 25 successful flights. (Mellins later acquired another claim to advertising fame when they engaged Humphrey Bogart's mother to design a poster and the infant superstar became the model for the gurgling Mellin-fed baby.)

Spencers signed the contract and took £1000, the first instalment of the money, in April 1902. They could now start work in their new airship workshop. This still stands in Highbury Grove, in essentially a similar state to its condition in 1902. It is the only black taxi repair shop listed Grade 2 by English Heritage.

The airship was completed in Islington and taken to Crystal Palace to live in an imposing shed. On the 23rd June the tall doors opened and an escort of aeronauts in nautical peaked caps and blue blazers brought out the airship to press and public. Messages about Mellins Baby Food covered its sides and its appearance was heralded everywhere as the all-British answer to Santos-Dumont.

Arthur Spencer took out a patent showing a silk airship envelope, 75 feet long by 20 feet in diameter, holding 20,000 cubic feet of hydrogen. A 'keel', a bamboo framework attached to

fig. 52. (left) Captain Alf Smith
fig. 53. (right) 'Countess' Ellen Smith, on the right of the picture

the envelope, supported the engine and a platform for the pilot to stand on. The pilot pulled ropes to control a mighty canvas rudder at the stern; an equally mighty 10 foot pinewood propeller, designed by Hiram Maxim, was at the front. The airship had a 3.5 horsepower British engine from Simms Manufacturing.

The airship needed to earn its keep. Visitors to Crystal Palace paid sixpence to watch it going round the Polo Ground with Stanley Spencer at the helm and Spencer aeronauts attending the ropes. One attendant, Alfred Smith, was known professionally as 'Captain' Smith and to his workmates as 'Smithy'. He had made many ascents and parachute jumps for the Spencers over the previous five years.

Smith's wife, Ellen, was also a parachutist, known as 'Countess S'. She learnt her trade with the Spencers in 1899 , and was not put off by a first jump that landed her on a railway line as a train approached. 'Before I could get off the lines, the buffer or some other part of the engine caught my shoulder and gave it a nasty knock. However, no real damage was done...' The Smiths also ran the 'Crown and Anchor' pub in Paul Street, Finsbury, just north of the City of London, inflated into 'The Balloon House, Finsbury' on their business cards. Alf Smith was to play an important part in the discomfiture of the Spencers over the Mellin airship experiment.

The *Westminster Gazette* described the airship's first flight. 'With Mr Stanley Spencer in the car, she sailed gracefully down the football field, wheeled round in a circle-a small circle, too-and perhaps for a quarter of an hour sailed a tortuous course over the heads of a small but enthusiastic crowd of spectators'.

On July 12th 1902 Stanley took up his nine year old niece, Marie. She was almost certainly the first female ever to fly in an airship. In her eighties she remembered it as not much of a

MR. AND MRS. SPENCER AND GLADYS SPENCER STANDING BY THE FLYING MACHINE IN WHICH THEY HAVE ALL JOURNEYED.

fig. 54. Stanley, Rose and their daughter, Gladys

flight, mostly consisting of being towed round with a rope. Her uncle wanted to check the airship's ability to carry more than an adult's weight and she was the right size. Her chief recollection was of embarrassment because her skirt kept blowing up.

The first long voyage of the airship took place on the 22nd September 1902. That afternoon Stanley travelled across London from Crystal Palace to Eastcote in north west London, a flight of about sixteen miles. L.T.C. Rolt commented, 'Spencer insisted he had perfect control of his machine throughout, but the curious gyrations he was seen to execute en route led spectators to the conclusion that he was not entirely the master of the light southerly breeze that was blowing at this time… this was a very courageous first flight for, as Santos-Dumont frankly admitted, he much preferred open fields to roof-tops when trying out his airships.'

The papers loved Stanley and his airship. A profile in the weekly *MAP* hailed 'A young-looking Englishman of thirty-four, shortish, broad-shouldered, lean-flanked, with light brown curling hair, a trifle sparse about the temples, a fiercely-pointed moustache, eyes of greyish-blue, strong-well cut features and a pale, clear and healthy complexion.' Stanley was the perfect Edwardian hero complete with a moustache so tightly twirled that you could clean a tobacco pipe with it. He was 'an enthusiastic photographer,… fond of athletics, cycling and motoring and is particularly devoted to fishing, much of the mechanism of the Mellin airship having been thought out on the banks of the Lea.'

Rose, Stanley's wife, was also popular. *MAP* described 'a plucky wife… Mrs Spencer shares her husband's confidence [about ballooning] which is just as well for her peace of mind. Like Mr Spencer, she is a record-breaker, being the first lady in the world to navigate an airship, as she did at the Crystal Palace, entirely alone in the car or steering platform.'

The airship went to Blackpool for a twenty-five mile flight in October and its fame grew through the rest of 1902. The airship's image was even pirated on advertisements for Audax, a cream for haemorrhoids and varicose veins made by Nyrdahl Products of Paris.

Publishers moved in on the act. Valentine and Tomlinson's *Travels in Space*, published that autumn, highlighted the airship; in December, John Bacon included several chapters on Spencers' exploits in *Dominion of the Air*, tracing the story back to the partnership of Edward Spencer and Charles Green. There were many photographs of the brothers' Highbury factory. It was all wonderful publicity.

The Spencers upgraded to their *No 2 Airship* during spring 1903. The increased weight of a 24 horsepower Simms engine required more lift, so the gasbag was enlarged to 93 feet long. At its first public flight the new airship jack-knifed and damaged its propeller. The show had to go on. As L.T.C. Rolt says, 'in order not to disappoint the spectators the resourceful aeronaut removed the engine and propeller and ascended as a free balloon.' By September, with everything repaired, the Spencers were ready to try for the prize.

Spencers had sought to persuade the Mellins' directors that their baby food had had sufficient exposure on the airship for them to hand over £500, the second and final instalment. Mellins were unimpressed and refused to pay up. Fortunately, the brothers found a new backer: *Evening News* was now emblazoned in huge letters along the sides of their new airship.

The newspaper proclaimed on Saturday, 12th September 1903: 'The *Evening News* airship. Look out for the St Paul's trip on Monday.' Readers may have looked out for the trip, but it never happened.

Various factors may have caused the postponement. The weather made this a difficult year for flight in England. Hugh Robert Mill told *The Times* on 29th October that '1903 is to prove the wettest year since Mr Symons established his first rain gauge in Camden Town.' Gipsy Hill Police Station had also given Spencers a stern warning about the perils that a flight over London could bring to the citizens beneath.

But they had to have a go. Their sponsors needed the publicity and they needed the money. At last, by 3.30pm on the following Thursday, everything was ready at Crystal Palace, but the weather was threatening, with dark clouds everywhere in the sky. Finally, at five minutes past five, the *Evening News* could see its airship and aeronaut off in heroic style. 'After kissing his little daughter, whom Mrs Spencer had brought to see her husband off, the aeronaut ordered the airship to be carried out into the air.'

Once 30,000 cubic feet of hydrogen had lifted the airship off the ground, Stanley started the engine and set off on the great adventure. He told the *Evening News* that he was concerned about weather conditions right from the beginning of the flight. He crossed South London from Sydenham to Peckham Rye (the first point from which he could see St Paul's because of the haze), then headed to a crossing of the Thames between Blackfriars and Waterloo Bridges.

The *Daily Mail*'s reporter was up on the dome of St Paul's with dozens of others, freezing in the 'stiff breeze' during the long wait. Spencer was expected at about 3.30pm and the fans and the curious in their thousands waited in the streets below.

William Claxton was among them. 'The writer remembers well moving among the dense crowds and hearing everywhere such remarks as these: "What would happen if a few bombs were thrown over the side of the air-ship?" "Will there be air-fleets in future, manned by the soldiers or sailors?" Indeed the uppermost thought in people's minds was not so much the possibility of Mr. Spencer being able to complete his journey successfully – nearly everyone recognised that air-ship construction had now advanced so far that it was only a matter of time for an ideal craft to be built – but that the coming of the air-ship was an affair of grave international importance.'

fig. 55. The crowd in St. Paul's Churchyard watching the airship

Finally, the watchers on the dome could see the airship. This is the *Mail*'s story: 'The afternoon was going grey and an old clock struck quarter past the hour of five – a little speck of black no bigger than a man's hand [was seen]. Now it stood bravely towards the summit of St Paul's and now, as its great canvas rudder was hauled over, it showed broadside on. (It swung round and round so quickly that it made one dizzy even to look at it). But swing as it did, it came on at a great pace, and only seconds might be counted between the time when it became distinct and when it was seen that Mr Spencer meant to pass to the eastwards of St Paul's.

The airship… must have been twice, or perhaps three times, the height of the golden cross… But far overhead as it was, the crowds… could see it clearly, traffic came to a standstill, and such a cheer rolled up as must have reached even Mr. Spencer.

Having got to northwards of the Cathedral, the aeronaut put his helm down, evidently aiming to go west and then beat up again to northwards to go round the dome. The airship, answering to the helm, came up quivering into the wind and the great propeller at the fore was going at racing speed. Then it paid off, as a horse jibs at a steep hill or a boat yaws at a stiff breeze. Again and again Mr. Spencer put down his helm and the airship came up quivering into the wind. But all the time it was drifting northwards.'

Stanley Spencer described how every time he brought the airship's nose round to go south the wind caught and blew it upwards. He estimated he was 800 feet above ground all this time and could hear the 'most inspiring' cheers of the crowds below as he fought the wind. He cut his hands on the steering rope in his efforts.

The *Mail*'s account concludes:

'For some twenty minutes Mr Spencer's battle with the breeze went on. It must have been a strong wind up there, for it was whistling round the dome of the cathedral. Then, evidently finding that he could make no headway, Mr Spencer put the head of his airship about, and with the wind astern of it and its propeller whisking round ahead of it, it drifted away like some toy kite lost in infinity. Then the darkness swallowed it up.'

Stanley flew right across London and landed in Trent Park, where he found some more fans. 'The Misses Bevan and other young ladies came up.' They were so enthusiastic that Stanley gave them a short trip round the park. While the Misses Bevan and their friends may have given Stanley's moustache a bit of lift at the end of the day, the flight was a terrible disappointment to him, his team and their backers.

Stanley pronounced himself satisfied with what had been achieved, claiming he had been struggling against a wind of fifteen to twenty miles per hour, and pointing out that Santos Dumont had made seven attempts before rounding the Eiffel Tower. The Spencers only had resources for one more try.

This time the airship travelled no further from Crystal Palace than Clapham Common before making a forced landing that ended dreams of the Northcliffe Prize. Spencers did not have the money or patronage of Count Zeppelin; they did not have Santos-Dumont's coffee bean millions.

The brothers were in trouble. On the 29th October 1903, Stanley, trading as Spencer Brothers, took Mellins Food to court for £500, which he claimed as the balance due of his agreed fee of £1500. Mellins counter-claimed. They wanted their one thousand pounds back.

The case came on earlier than expected and Mr Justice Darling, sitting with a jury, honed his wit on Cyril Dodd, KC, Stanley's barrister. Mr Dodd said his witnesses would not be there before twelve o'clock. The judge responded, 'I see your client is the proprietor of a balloon. Will he be coming in that?' Mr Dodd, a bit disloyally, replied 'I think not, otherwise I should not be so positive he would be here at twelve o' clock.'

Darling told him to open his case pending the arrival of witnesses.

So counsel explained that when Santos-Dumont was trying to go round the Eiffel Tower, 'Mellin's Food, moved thereto by patriotism, and a desire to sell their food, got into communication with the plaintiffs, who were engaged in building a navigable balloon... to beat Santos-Dumont.' For £1500 the plaintiffs were to advertise 'Mellin's Food' in dark blue letters six foot ten inches high, on each side of 'Our British Navigable Balloon'; make 25 'return journeys' during the period of the contract; and carry 'advertising matter' for Mellins Food to be used in lieu of ordinary sand or water ballast.

Stanley Spencer had by then arrived. He told the court that on September 19th 1902, he had travelled to Harrow 'making several circles over London'. He also threw out advertisements for Mellins Food from the balloon. The judge asked, 'Was there a great scramble for them?' Stanley : 'Oh, yes, there was great excitement' (laughter).

When cross-examined, Stanley was emphatic that he 'did not go with the wind to Harrow', in other words, that his balloon was truly navigable. Furthermore, while at Crystal Palace, 'It was not true that there was always a number of men holding on to the trail rope and lugging the balloon along.' Percy Spencer gave evidence in support of his brother.

Mr Bliss, the chairman of Mellin's Food, appeared in the witness box. The judge was now enjoying himself. 'I cannot see why anybody, infant or not, should buy a packet of Mellin's Food because Mellins own a navigable balloon.' This got a laugh so he replayed an edited version. 'Why should a person say Mellin is the owner of a navigable balloon therefore I will buy a packet of babyfood?' (More laughter)

Mr Bliss was up to the challenge. 'We advertise on airships or anything else to bring our name before the public… ' Mr Bliss had seen the first ascent of the balloon from Crystal Palace and told the court, 'It was taken out of a building and was held by several people. The screw revolved for a short time, and then the balloon was taken back.' (Laughter). Mr Bliss had complained to the Spencers. They undertook to carry out the promised journeys as soon as practicable. Mellins felt Stanley had not fulfilled the contract, but would now pay him the £500 if he made a return journey over London.

Spencers' counsel suggested to Bliss that publicity was the issue, not the performance of the airship.

Mr Dodd: 'All you wanted was an advertisement.'
The witness: 'Yes.'
Mr Dodd: 'Well, you are getting a splendid one now.'
The witness: 'I do not know, Sir.' (Laughter)

Mr Dodd argued that the airship had been around the Crystal Palace grounds 53 times so the contract for 25 flights had been exceeded. Eldon Bankes, KC, for the defendants, would have none of this. 'It only left Crystal Palace grounds once and was then taken back in a cart.'

There was devastating evidence to come. We have met Alfred Smith as one of the aeronauts looking after the first airship at Crystal Palace. He now stepped up as a witness for Mellins. He claimed that he and a ground crew had towed the airship round the polo ground at Crystal Palace to give the impression that it was navigable. 'It was not a navigable balloon at any time it was at the Palace. I had a conversation with Mr Spencer about it, and I was given to understand that it would not come back by its motive power. So when it did go away I had to go to the works to tell Mr Percival Spencer, and he made preparations to get it back to the works. It was an ordinary balloon and nothing more.' According to the newspapers, this speech raised roars of laughter in court.

Stanley's lawyers tried to discredit Alfred Smith:

'The defendants [Mellins] approached the witness two days ago on the matter [of appearing as a witness]. He then went and told Mr Spencer, and asked him to pay what was due to him, but did not say that if he did not he would give evidence for Mellins.'

But debate quickly returned to the airship's outings and Alf Smith was back in his element.

Mr Dodds: 'Would not the balloon go at an angle to the wind?'
Witness: 'Yes – if the wind was at the angle '(Laughter)
Mr Dodds: 'You say it went round the Polo Ground at Crystal Palace -it must have gone at an angle then.'
Witness: 'Yes, but we did the angling.' (Laughter)

In the end Stanley was not awarded his £500; but the court was unsympathetic to Mellins' counter-claim for £1000 and allowed Spencers to keep what they had received.

The story of how Alfred Smith, who led the team looking after the 1902 airship, changed sides and attacked the Spencers in court survived by chance. The usual sources do not mention the action. Smith, or his wife, collected newspaper reports of the case in a scrapbook which was sold, probably after Ellen Smith's death in the 1930s, at the Caledonian Market in North London. It eventually came up in a Sotheby's sale in the 1980s where I was able to buy it.

fig. 56. The monument to Alfred and Ellen Smith in East Finchley Cemetery

The cuttings show that Smith had left the Spencers' employment by October 1903. A parachute accident in which he and his 'Countess' were involved in June 1903 almost certainly played a part in his change of loyalties. In a jump at Pontypridd (Wales again!) a cross wind pushed the Smiths well away from the safe dropping ground. Ellen had the better luck. She came down in a tree, so rescuers could get a ladder to her and bring her to safety.

But poor Alf fell on some telegraph wires high – some reports said 50 feet (15 metres) high) – over a shallow section of the river Taff. The ladder was not long enough to help. He hung desperately to the wires, cutting his hands deeply in the process, but eventually had to let go and fell heavily onto the riverbed. Helpers pulled him out unconscious with a broken pelvis. His boss, Percy Spencer, as reported in the *Leader* newspaper, was not unduly sympathetic. 'Mr Spencer said that Capt. Smith knew his business thoroughly. If there was an error, it was perhaps a mistake to go up without a wind to carry them clear of any obstructions.' Smith obviously felt the Spencers owed him money at the time of the court case. Perhaps a lack of adequate, or any, compensation after the accident led to the rift.

Smith recovered fully from his injuries but was now out of a job. He could hardly return to Spencers after events in court. Only Short Brothers in Battersea Park and Auguste Gaudron at the Alexandra Palace needed aeronauts. In the end Gaudron took him on.

'Countess S' seems to have never parachuted again; Ellen Smith managed the Crown and Anchor while her husband was touring. Alf Smith worked for Gaudron for several years and sent brief reports to his wife at the pub. He wrote this postcard from the York Gala showground, probably in June 1909.

My dear Wiff

Received your Letter. Pleased everything is allright. Having very fine weather here. Very Hot. now getting Balloon ready for Captive Work. HTQ [abbreviation for a balloon's name] being filled for me at 4.30 have got two Passengers up till now. Let me have another Letter with fondest Love Hubby

Dolly Shepherd, in her marvellous book about parachuting for Auguste Gaudron, *When The 'Chute Went Up*, implies that Smith met with another serious accident that finished his parachuting career for good. 'From time to time a member of our team might 'disappear'… if questioned, Captain Gaudron would merely say that the aeronaut in question had 'left the team.' They had left sure enough! …Devil-may-care Captain Smith and handsome, dashing Captain Fleet-they 'disappeared…'

'Devil-may-care' Smith survived whatever accident made him 'disappear', but the end of his life was far from happy. He killed himself by swallowing potassium cyanide on the 3rd April 1914. His Countess died much later, in 1936. Visitors often notice their grave with its relief of a parachutist in the St. Pancras and Islington Cemetery, East Finchley, London.

The court action finished Stanley Spencer financially. He appeared in the Court of Bankruptcy in February 1904. Stanley told the receiver that 'The balloons and airships were the property of his brother's firm, from whom he hired them as occasion required… Of his present indebtedness, £558 was due to his brother's firm for hire of balloons and airships, and £154 for law costs [from the case against Mellins]'.

Troubled times for the Spencers were not at an end. Developments that would make airships redundant for most purposes were taking shape as the Wright Brothers perfected their machines. But the Wrights' achievements had less immediate impact on the Spencers than the sudden death, at the age of 59, of their patron, friend and public relations asset, the Reverend John Bacon. He died, after a short illness, on Christmas Day, 1904. Percy was one of those who carried his coffin.

While attending Bacon's funeral, Percy would have known that another, more personal, tragedy would not be long delayed. His wife, Mary, had been ill with abdominal cancer for eighteen months. She died less than two months later, on the 7th February 1905.

There was now no-one to care for Marie the little aeronaut, who was then 11, her three sisters and her brother when their father was at work. So their grandmother, Louise, Charles Green Spencer's widow, took matters in hand. She descended on Percy's six bedroom house and ran the place, according to Marie Townend, with a firm, and not always popular, hand.

There was more sadness to come. By November 1905 Stanley was back in India. He unwisely told the *Daily Mail* that he was taking out a large balloon so that the Prince of Wales, who was making a royal tour at the same time, could 'have a birds-eye view of some of the principal cities of India.' The Prince's minders took a dim view of the announcement and Percy, as head of the firm, was forced to contradict his younger brother publicly. In the end, Stanley just made captive balloon flights and three balloon flights as part of the Olympia Exhibition at Calcutta (Kolkata): the expedition was not a success. He headed for home in January on the steamer *City of Benares*, but contracted typhoid fever and was taken off the ship at Valletta Harbour, Malta.

Stanley died in the Central Hospital, Valletta, on the 26th January 1906. He was 36 years old. *The Daily Mirror* described him as 'the alert and intrepid young aeronaut, whose exploits have earned him an assured place in the history of the conquest of the air'. The rest of the English press followed this line: Stanley Spencer was a great British hero.

Rose, his wife, emigrated to America shortly afterwards and married a man called Elmer Reed.

fig. 57. The French fortified town of Gravelines, photographed by Percy. Courtesy the Spencer family

fig. 58. Preparing the valve. Courtesy the Spencer family

X

Just airborne

In four short years C. G. Spencer and Sons had gone from the heights of prestige to the depleted enterprise that mourned Stanley's death in 1906.

But much was still going right. The partners were winning headlines with adventurous flights. Eight Spencer parachutists barnstormed the country during the summer, moving from fair to gala to Bank Holiday spectacular from weekend to weekend.

The relationship with influential members of the Aero Club remained strong. Frank Hedges Butler was a good friend. He and Percy each received a handsome medal from the Club for a long flight from London to Caen in France on 30th August 1905. The expedition provided exciting aerial photographs for Percy's lantern slide shows.

Arthur superintended preparations in February 1906 for the Channel crossing by Pollock and Dale, two other Club members, in the big Spencer-built balloon *Vivienne III*. The aeronauts reached France safely. They appreciated the new Spencer 'instant' ripcord which allowed rapid deflation of the balloon when it landed in a gale and snowstorm and left them muddy but unscathed: only their hats were wrecked.

While amateur ballooning was booming, many pioneers in lighter-than-air craft were turning their attention to aircraft. Santos-Dumont, for example, was developing a biplane in 1906 and had left airships behind.

The demand for professional balloon pilots declined as the amateurs learnt fast through games such as the 'Point to Point', won by landing nearest to a prearranged point. As many as thirty balloons sometimes took part in the racing, so the Club laid a twelve inch gas main specially for balloon inflation at the Hurlingham Club.

H. Massac Buist described an international 'Point to Point' as a passenger in *Vivienne III*, with Griffith Brewer as pilot. Their competitors included Her Serene Highness Princess Blucher from Germany and the ubiquitous Mrs Assheton Harbord in the *Valkyrie*. The crew had specialist local knowledge. 'Sir Claude [de Crespigny was]… the self-appointed

fig. 59. Her Serene Highness Princess Blucher ready for take off

honorary lookout man, than whom none could have been better chosen... in that hereabout was all his own country, every hedge and ditch was familiar to him through hunting.'

One balloon came down in Stratford in London's East End. The balloon envelope swayed against the side of a house and vented gas into an upper room. 'A man called Belcher calmed the alarmed mother and child who were the only occupants of the room..."Stratford is not the best part of England," observed one of the competitors. "The people there are rather common, and keep asking for money."'

The amateurs took these competitions seriously. Harry Harper tells how Griffith Brewer spent the night before a 'Point to Point' in his balloon basket. He wanted to make an early morning study of wind currents before the formation of clouds in lower strata obscured those higher in the sky.

It worked. Brewer managed to land his balloon just over a mile away from the target the judges had set near Maidenhead in Berkshire, miles from the start at Hurlingham. His observations had allowed him to set his balloon's height precisely where the wind currents would do him the most good.

The first Gordon Bennett Balloon Race from Paris in 1906 boosted aeronautical enthusiasm further.

By now the leading British contender was Charlie Rolls, who flew across the Channel to Sandringham in Norfolk and took third place. Significantly for Spencers' reputation, Rolls had bought his balloon *Britannia* (complete with electric light) from Short Brothers. Rolls had also bought balloons that year from Gaudron and Mallet in Paris.

According to *Balloons and Ballooning*, Shorts took the prestigious Aero Club contract from Spencers shortly after that race. The authors explained: 'Members of the club became unhappy with the quality and stability (due to the shape used) of the Spencer balloons and contacted the rival Short Brothers whose balloons were influenced by French design and whose quality was considered superior.' The brothers involved in C. G. Spencer and Sons were no longer the dominant force in English balloon manufacture.

Rolls was not just a rich aristocrat. He was an engineer who had learned his craft practically and theoretically at Cambridge University. John Moore-Brabazon, an early aviator who later became Lord Brabazon of Tara and gave his name to one of the most enormous aircraft ever made, also studied engineering at Cambridge and worked for Rolls in the vacations.

Moore-Brabazon made his feelings about English balloon design clear at a meeting hosted by the Committee of the Automobile Club on the 18th February 1904.

'he thought it a pity none of the English manufacturers [presumably Spencer and Gaudron] *tried to keep up-to-date. They had never – up to the present – tried the ballonet* [a device used to maintain constant height], *and the valve employed by them was the same type as that in use on balloons at the Siege of Paris* [in 1870].*'*

But Rolls' behaviour towards the Spencers puzzled Brabazon. 'I never quite got to the bottom of why he disapproved of this firm…but he disliked the pear-shaped balloons they made and was always anxious to get hold of somebody else to make the perfectly spherical model such as had been introduced in France.' Brabazon claimed that Rolls persuaded the French manufacturer Mallet to show Short Brothers how to make the spherical models.

There was no commercial pressure on the barnstorming aeronauts to innovate: Spencers simply needed a working parachute and a balloon to draw crowds at county shows and galas. The *Shrewsbury Chronicle* recorded total show takings of £3,043.75 in a full page description of the local Great Floral and Musical Show in August 1905 and commented 'It is marvellous to observe the continued interest which visitors to the fete, as well as the townsfolk, continue to take in the aeronautical programme which is year by year submitted to them.'

The Times of 5th April 1904 reported that 78,031 people passed through the Crystal Palace turnstiles on Easter Bank Holiday. 'Mr Spencer's successful balloon ascent in the afternoon attracted thousands of spectators.' On the same day, on the other side of London, 70,000 paid to enter the Alexandra Palace grounds. 'At 2.30 there was a balloon ascent by M. Gaudron and Captain Stringer, the balloon sailing away in fine style to the south-east.' Dolly Shepherd tells us that entry to these events was normally one shilling, reducing to sixpence as the end of the event became nearer. The organisers certainly had the resources to pay a reasonable performance fee.

Rolls and his friends, the innovators, were always competing; they wanted cars, balloons or aeroplanes to outdo their rivals, and could afford to indulge their enthusiasms. Their rivalry drove forward the development of balloons, as it did every other technology that their interest touched.

A few soldiers were also chasing the very best. Colonel Capper of the Farnborough military balloon establishment, who visited the Wright Brothers in 1904, was passionate about aeronautical progress.

The two packs hunted together. The programme for the Hurlingham Club's balloon contest on the 24th June 1908 records that 'At 4.45pm balloons are scheduled to ascend for the 'Hare and Hounds' race for the Rolls Trophy, presented by the Hon.C.S. Rolls. Twenty four individuals made up the eleven crews listed as 'Hounds'. Eight of them were army officers, including Capper and three other officers from the Royal Engineers. Charlie Rolls in his balloon *Imp* was naturally 'The Hare'.

The links went far beyond casual acquaintance. Capper and Rolls were friends and Rolls was a part-time soldier. Capper is said to have tipped Rolls off about the quality of Short Brothers' workmanship. Rolls took his girlfriend Sylvia Assheton-Harbord to visit Shorts at their workshops just off Tottenham Court Road. They were impressed.

Finally, as with the airship experiments, amateurs like Rolls, and to some extent the soldiers, had the resources to test and re-test ideas and equipment. Spencer Brothers had little capital and a relatively slim income.

At one point, Henry Spencer worked with Auguste Gaudron on a prototype military airship. Dr Barton of Beckenham was building a 'trial battle craft' to a War Office specification, as a British version of Count Zeppelin's dirigibles.

The Barton craft was constructed in a purpose-built shed behind the Alexandra Palace. William Claxton lived nearby: 'The huge balloon was 43 feet in diameter and 176 feet long, with a gas capacity of 235,000 cubic feet. To maintain the external form of the envelope a smaller balloon, or compensator, was placed inside the larger one. The framework was of bamboo, and the car was attached by about eighty wire-cables. The wooden deck was about 123 feet in length. Two 50-horse-power engines drove four propellers, two of which were at either end.'

The first flight was delayed and delayed again, though visitors could pay three pence to view the great craft. But then *The Times* (4.7.1904) reported: 'Dr Barton…met with a somewhat serious accident early yesterday morning.' Harry Spencer and Dr Barton were working late, making stocks of hydrogen in large retorts. 'A loud explosion was heard about 2.15am and Mr Spencer found Dr Barton by the side of one of the retorts …It is believed that Dr Barton, finding that one of the generators had ceased to work, although it had only recently been charged had the lid removed and fed in some more iron… by some means a spark must have come in contact with the gaseous mixture and caused the explosion.' Barton was lucky not to lose his sight. He took months to recover and by then the 1904 flying season was over.

Later still, the airship's envelope was somehow ripped against the hangar wall. William Claxton found all this frustrating. '…for months we were doomed to disappointment; something always seemed to go wrong at the last minute…'

Finally on July 22nd, Barton, his collaborator Rawson, Auguste Gaudron and Harry Spencer, who took a little dog with him for luck, embarked on the airship. They wore yachting dress, complete with peaked caps and blue blazers. Each had a parachute in case the craft got into difficulties, a facility only permitted to British military aeroplane pilots at the very end of the First World War.

The airship sailed off towards East London. Barton reported that they could navigate the airship in 20mph winds, but when the wind became stronger, as it did towards the end of the afternoon, such steering became impossible. Colonel Capper, the official army observer, was less impressed. He later reported to his superiors that the airship was only making 3 to 5 mph progress against an 18 mph wind, so was actually drifting at 13 to 15 mph.

The airship flew out over Wood Green, Lea Bridge and Romford. The wind grew stronger. The aeronauts decided to land in a field just past Romford. The touch down, overseen by Gaudron, was perfect. Barton reported, 'The bamboo deck on which we were standing alighted in the field without so much as a jerk'. So now 176 feet of airship was on the ground, tugged at by the wind.

fig. 60. (left) The Barton-Rawson airship
fig. 61. (right) Auguste Gaudron

Your view of what happened next will be coloured by the account you choose. The air-friendly *Daily Mail* burbled 'London Airship's Voyage First Successful Trip.' But even the *Mail* published Barton's account of the wreck.

'Forgetful of balance, the four of us gathered together in the bow, with the result that the stern of the ship mounted rapidly in the air till it was forty feet or so from the ground. Mr Spencer sprang up the framework and pulled the 'ripping valve' which cuts a hole in the balloon. The gas began to rush out with a roar, and its force split the balloon exactly in halves. There was a roar like thunder, the balloon collapsed and the framework came crashing to the ground. None of us were hurt…'

According to the *Press*, Barton said, 'There goes five years' work and £4000' as he left his experiment. The *Mail* talked of his starting on a heavier-than-air craft. It never happened. War Office interest had ended even before the crash. Without knowing how the voyage ended, Capper's report damned the airship: 'The ship is of no practical utility whatsoever.'

So neither Gaudrons or Spencers broke out of the round of galas into the big time. They went on hiring, touring, ballooning and parachuting from their bases in the peoples' palaces of north and south London.

Gaudron made record-breaking balloon flights to Sweden in 1906. Percy Spencer crossed the Channel several times, and accompanied Mrs Griffith Brewer and Frank Hedges Butler in February 1906 from Wandsworth and Putney Gas Works to Samer near Boulogne. Mrs Griffith Brewer, the first woman to make the crossing, told the *Daily News* that she 'trusted that ballooning would become more popular with the fair sex.'

fig. 62. Percy, with Miss Godwynne Earle, advertising the 'balloon cure' for overworked actresses

By summer 1906, the press had discerned a new trend for the rich: the ballooning weekend. Percy saw an opening and launched 'the balloon cure'. The *Evening News* reported how a Spencer balloon flew Miss Godwynne Earle, an actress and impressionist who starred in the Coliseum Revue, with two friends from Highbury to Normandy. Percy declared when they got back to Charing Cross Station 'the balloon cure for the nerves is going to be fashionable… the delightful sensation of floating in the air acts likes a dew-bandage. I have a fleet of eighteen balloons, any one of which I will place at your service for £20… The wealthy classes are taking up the cure with enthusiasm.' Miss Godwynne Earle backed him up. 'I am going on another trip next weekend, for I think Mr Spencer's cure is just lovely, and I feel awfully well just now.' Her curves and those of the balloon, along with Percy and his beard, appeared all over the popular papers that weekend.

The idea caught on. George Bernard Shaw booked a £20 flight with Spencers from Wandsworth Gas Works for the afternoon of the 3rd July, 1906. Percy took GBS, Granville Barker, Robert Loraine and his sister-in-law up to 9000 feet in a two hour flight. Loraine, who combined an interest in aviation with performances in Shaw's and other plays, wrote it was 'very pleasant and seraphic with nothing happening, except that Shaw would peer through a hole in the boarding at his feet which made him rather sick. We discussed landing… I thought the people would be rather interested to receive visitors from the air, and especially flattered when they discovered Shaw's identity. "Don't be so certain," said Shaw. "They may think my works detestable." 'In the event', says Michael Holroyd, 'they bumped down in a field near Chobham and were met by a purple-faced landowner, unacquainted with Shaw's oeuvre but waving a shooting-stick.' Loraine explained, 'the welcome he gave us was a curt direction as to the quickest way off his property.'

Michael Holroyd suggests that Shaw gave Percy Spencer theatrical immortality in the play *Misalliance* in which an airman called Joey Percival crashes his plane into the Tarleton family's greenhouse. The Tarletons have a large house in fashionable Hindhead, Surrey, built on the success of the family lingerie business, Tarleton's Underwear.

Joey Percival is suitably apologetic to his host about the damage.

The aviator: I'm really very sorry. I've knocked your vinery into a cocked hat. You don't mind, do you?
Tarleton: Not a bit. Come in and have some tea. Stay to dinner. Stay over the weekend.
All my life I've wanted to fly.
The aviator: You're really more than kind.

Michael Holroyd is almost certainly wrong: Joey Percival, except in name, is not much like Percival Spencer. He is a rich and Oxford-educated young man. Percy was a short, stoutish, middle-aged aeronaut.

Joey has with him a passenger who, once unwrapped from flying gear, turns out to be a woman. The daredevil feminist ex machina is called Lina Szczepanowska (the latter pronounced, as she explains to the awestruck household, with Sz as in fish and Cz as in church). She warns that 'Rome fell. Babylon fell. Hindhead's turn will come,' and turns the country house comedy of the first half of the play into anarchy by its end. After a 50 line speech advocating freedom for women, she leaves carrying a would-be assassin, who has been found hiding in a portable Turkish bath, over one shoulder.

Joey may not be much like Percy, but it is hard not to associate Lina with the powerful knickerbockered figures of Dolly Shepherd and the other women parachutists of the day. Shaw seems to be using flight, which transforms the view of all that goes on below, as a metaphor for the transformation of society that he hoped to see.

Suffragism, air travel and the Spencers came together in real life in February 1909. Muriel Matters was from Australia, where women already had the vote. She planned a leaflet bombing of the Westminster area when King Edward VII came to open Parliament. Henry Spencer was in charge of the airship that would carry her over London.

'I had already won my spurs by chaining myself to the grille of the ladies gallery in the House of Commons. As a result of this I was intrusted with the aerial demonstration on the day of the opening of parliament. That morning I went to Hendon and met Mr Henry Spencer who had his airship all ready near the Welsh Harp. It was quite a little airship, 80 feet long, and written in large letters on the gas bag were three words, Votes For Women.'

In 2002, Marian Sawer, of the Australian National University, told the National Labor Women's Conference the end of the story. 'Air currents had taken her up to about 3,500 feet, so she was unable to use her megaphone to address the parliamentarians. She did, however, scatter the 56 pounds of handbills she had taken with her. She told the *Daily Mirror*: 'We were throwing down bills all the time, yellow, green and white (the colours of the Women's Freedom League) — they floated down to the people below like beautifully coloured birds.'

Meanwhile the other Spencer brothers were preparing their stand for the first London Aero Show at Olympia. *Flight* was jubilant, 'The nineteenth of March 1909 will be a memorable day in the history for British aviation.' Shorts and the French aeroplane manufacturers were making the running; Spencers were still showing balloons and airships.

They had one piece of free publicity, though they may not have appreciated it. *Flight* included a cartoon entitled: 'Spencers' balloons – Mary gives her little lamb a blowing up'. The drawing shows a little girl blowing up a lamb-shaped balloon, in front of Spencers' show stand. The stand holds other little balloons, including one in the shape of an elephant: all good fun but hardly likely to link the Spencer brand with the cutting edge of aeronautics.

Mr. Herbert Spencer, who has just qualified for his pilot's certificate at Brooklands, on a biplane constructed by himself.

fig. 63. Herbert Spencer and his biplane in 1911

Something had to change. The youngest brother, Herbert, had had a motor car driving licence since 1903. He was enthusiastic and knowledgeable about the new auto and aero technologies. The firm went into partnership with the French motor company, Berliet, to exploit Herbert's expertise.

So at the 1910 Olympia Aero Show, the Spencers were able to show a monoplane designed by Herbert Spencer and a W. Stirling on the Berliet stand. You could buy this 27 foot long aircraft with its two propellers, 34ft wing span and top speed of 40 miles per hour for £650. While this was a move in the right direction, the plane 'was not a success and there were no further reports after the Show; the engine was used in a later aircraft.'

Herbert moved to a base in Shed 9, at Brooklands Flying Grounds in Surrey, to build a biplane. He tested his new model in November 1910 and had fully refined the plane, a two seater with a 50HP Gnome engine, by July 1911. Once his plane was built, Herbert could finish teaching himself to fly, and was awarded his Aviator's Certificate (no. 124) on 29th August 1911. He then went on to teach others and was often to be seen above Brooklands putting his pupils through their paces.

Flight described the aircraft: 'His machine is an exceptionally fine one of its type, its chief points being that of high speed and delicacy of control. It is also apparently very stable, only a slight, almost imperceptible, movement of the control lever being necessary.' Sadly someone called Hawkins wrecked this biplane beyond repair in February 1912.

Herbert was successful in competition at Brooklands in 1913. This time he was flying a

fig. 64. Ancient and modern: the carthorse and the biplane

plane, originally named the MacFie Empress, that he had improved with features of his favourite Farman design.

Charles Turner flew with him. 'Among the aviators at Brooklands was Mr Herbert Spencer with whom I had many flights. He was a junior member of the third generation of the famous ballooning family. He had a biplane of his own design and construction, and taught many pupils and gave innumerable passenger flights. His machine was lighter than the average biplane of its class, and was faster than the ordinary Farman.'

Turner, writing in 1927, had collapsed all Herbert's plane-building into just one model. Herbert completed four planes, including a last one built just after the start of the First World War in August 1914. *Flight* reported on the 9th October 1914, 'It was almost like old times up at Hendon last Saturday week, for the weather was ideal, and there was a small but interested gate, whilst several machines were to be seen out on the aerodrome… W. F. Merriam tested a new Spencer biplane. This machine is like a miniature Henry Farman, and has a very business-like appearance.'

The Admiralty controlled more aircraft than the Royal Flying Corps at the beginning of World War 1. It requisitioned Herbert's aircraft, christened it *Admiralty 200* and used it as a trainer for a year or so. Then the technology moved on and the Spencer biplane and the name of Herbert Spencer dropped out of the story of aircraft building for good.

Earthbound, Herbert became the Metropolitan Police ju-jitsu instructor and ran the Highbury Barn pub in Islington near the ground of his favourite team, Arsenal Football Club.

fig. 65. The destruction of a kite balloon by a German aeroplane, Doiran Front.
William. T. Wood, 1917. Courtesy Imperial War Museum © IWM

— • XI • —

Spencers in the First World War

Percival Spencer and Auguste Gaudron both died in 1913. Percy was buried in a tomb in East Finchley Cemetery topped by a magnificent stone balloon. Gaudron was buried in Highgate Cemetery in Charles Green Spencer's family grave.

Auguste Gaudron's company died with him. His wife, Marina, went to the United States later in the year with her daughter, Victorine (Ena) who gives us a flavour of the life: 'Mama must have been quite a gal, did everything the boys did, fancy gymnastics (doesn't seem so long ago since she used to scare me with tricks like dropping flat on her face for fun & of course she knew how to land) monkeys and snakes for pets, no wonder she was such a good pioneer in Montana, driving a hay wagon at harvest, killing skunks that prowled under her flat and thought nothing of being alone, nearest neighbour mile or so away, 30 miles from town. And I am such a cream puss physically.'

Cream puss or not, she took after her mother in one sense: they married the brothers Hugh and Arthur Hampton. Hugh Hampton was 21 years younger than Marina, but there was only just over a year between Ena and Arthur.

Arthur Spencer, the second son, succeeded Percy as managing director at C.G. Spencer and Sons. As we have seen, Henry, the fourth brother, had broken away from the firm in the early 1900s (or had been pushed out, according to Marie Townend) and joined the experimenters around Auguste Gaudron at the Alexandra Palace. Henry worked with Gaudron on several airships besides the Barton project. After Gaudron's death, Henry and Arthur seem to have made common cause in work for the armed services.

By the end of 1914, Henry was attached to the Royal Naval Air Station at Farnborough. The Royal Naval Air Service (RNAS) then controlled all 'lighter-than-air' craft, including airships and observation balloons. Major Maitland, who was in charge of this corner of the Allied war effort, had flown with Auguste Gaudron and Charles Turner on the longest ever balloon flight from England. After travelling 1117 miles the aeronauts landed in Russia, where local

— • 105 • —

officials locked them up as spies. Fortunately the chief of gendarmerie, who understood about balloon flights, arranged their release and a luncheon in their honour.

Maitland probably knew Henry through his work with Gaudron; he would certainly have had to approve Henry's attachment to the small experimental team at Farnborough. Henry did his bit in introducing the parachute to the British forces just before Christmas 1914. The officer commanding RNAS Kingsnorton wrote enthusiastically to the Director, Air Department (abbreviated to DAD), on the 23rd December .

'...Mr Spencer of Messrs Spencer Bros...arrived [here] on the 17th inst. with two of his patent parachutes. He was anxious to give a personal exhibition of their use, so after the necessary authority had been obtained, at 2.25 pm No 3 Airship carried out an ascent for this purpose. The parachute container was triced up [secured] immediately astern of the airship car. There was a strong wind blowing, namely about twenty five miles on the ground and thirty five to forty miles an hour at a height of a thousand feet. The airship proceeded to a height of a thousand feet and placed herself in a position selected by Mr Spencer with a view to his landing on suitable ground.*

Mr Spencer then caught hold of the sides of the slip of the parachute, placed his legs in the slings and jumped off. The parachute appeared to open after a drop of hundred feet or less. Mr Spencer came gently and safely to earth and landed with so little shock that, though he lost his balance on touching the ground owing to the speed of the wind, he only had to touch the ground gently with one hand to steady himself. He landed in rather a muddy field so that if he had made anything of a bad landing, the fact would have been evident from the appearance of his clothes. It was noticeable also that he landed at almost exactly the point for which he was aiming.

Previous to seeing this experiment, I had never [seen?] any parachute work, and I regarded parachutes as clumsy and unreliable. This experiment has completely changed my views. The weight of the entire parachute is only 28 pounds and it is extremely neat as to stowage and quite as safe as most operations of aeronautics.

Though I do not wish in this report to make any recommendations, I consider there is probably a very extended field of utility for this apparatus.

I have the honour to be, Sir, your obedient servant,

R. Usborne
Wing Commander '

M.F. Sueter, D.A.D. himself, sent an order on the 7th January 1915 that Spencers should tender for the supply of twelve more parachutes. But some dinosaurs still opposed the introduction of parachutes as standard escape equipment, even from balloons. Maitland decided on a personal demonstration. Alan Morris describes his jump in a Spencer parachute at the Roehampton Polo Ground, another RNAS balloon centre.

'Two years later [Major] Maitland would be admitted to the Distinguished Service Order, but not for his Staff Work. That coveted decoration was really won the morning he went up from Roehampton and stopped the winch at 2000ft.'

Spencer parachutes were 'fixed line': when Maitland jumped, a line attached to his harness tugged the parachute out of an acorn-shaped bag.

'With a muffled explosion and a slight jerk on his harness the silk billowed into a canopy, and Maitland calmly timed his six-minute descent. As he hung seesawing he had no control over direction. Carried *past the dropping zone he thumped into and skittled a line of Inns of Court riflemen drilling in the grounds of Baron Rothschild's Roehampton House.*

But his experiment had ensured that no balloonist would be lost for want of C. G. Spencer's Static-Line (Automatic) Parachute. Although Maitland was to make many more drops, some under fire, in terms of morale building and man-power conservation this was the most momentous parachute descent of the war.'

The sceptics now had to concede that the parachute was a safe device for escape from static airships and balloons.

In 1914 the British services only had spherical balloons, which could spin wildly when tethered and provided a poor platform for observation, let alone the health of an observer. The Germans had solved this problem years earlier with the development of the sausage-shaped 'kite balloon', designed for stable flying into a wind, on the principle of a kite. The Royal Naval Air Service sent Arthur off to Belgium to look at a German-built kite balloon. He came back with notes and made a prototype.

Once the prototype was approved, the Admiralty ordered full production. The balloon was just part of the kit: winches, valves, cables and gas-making equipment and parachutes were also required. Demand from the Admiralty soon exceeded Spencers' capacity, even with a substantial increase in staff, so three other companies, Airships, Vickers and Mandlebergs of Manchester were brought in. The firms kept the British supplied with kite balloons until the end of the war.

In November 1915 Maitland put on his Spencer parachute again. While the crew of the Barton airship had had parachutes in 1903, few senior officers in 1915 accepted their life-saving potential for those travelling in a moving craft. William Claxton described the jump.

'With the dirigible travelling at about 20 miles an hour the major [Maitland] climbed over the car and seated himself in the parachute. Then it became detached from the Delta and shot downwards for about 200 feet at a terrific rate. For a moment or two it was thought that the opening apparatus had failed to work; but gradually the 'umbrella' opened, and the gallant major had a gentle descent for the rest of the distance.' Lord Edward Grosvenor, who was attached to the Royal Flying Corps, watched the descent. He said: 'Major Maitland has proved the practicability of members of an air-ship's crew dropping to the ground if the necessity arises.'

Both sides were now exploiting kite balloons tethered high above the trenches for observation and artillery direction. Observers could see for miles, judge enemy movements and report by telephone to their commanders.

Once they understood the balloons' potential, the English, French and German commanders increased the numbers deployed and ordered anti-aircraft gunners and air forces to destroy the blimps of their opponents. Some pilots became addicted to 'balloon-busting' as they discovered the explosive possibilities of hydrogen gas in the balloon envelopes. An observer without a parachute had no chance if the balloon was shot up and caught fire.

The adventures of Lieutenant Jolley of the Second Kite Balloon Wing give an idea of the risks. Enemy action forced Jolley to jump from his balloon on seven occasions between May and June 1917. Overall the Wing's observers made 106 emergency jumps during that year.

Maitland's jumps and Spencers' parachutes made the job of the British balloon observer, the 'balloonatic', slightly more tolerable. In contrast, French kite balloon observers were not allowed to take up parachutes until a good way into the war and suffered heavy casualties as a result. The Germans also lost many observers before 1916 when the Paulus parachute came into mass-production and general use.

J.H.Dundas-Grant, explained the induction of a balloonatic in the *Aerostat* magazine in

December 1983. Training was short, but recruits at least learned to pilot a free balloon in case they found themselves in one that broke loose from its tether.

'We were launched from Hurlingham and usually floated out over London. Our pilot would regale us with stories of his peace-time flights, while we amused ourselves writing stamped and addressed postcards and dropping them over the side. Two of mine reached their destination.'

The training finished with a solo flight in a small balloon.

'It was good fun coming down and chatting to the people below. We had to stay up an hour and did not usually prolong it because, as soon as we had landed and packed up, we were at liberty to go on leave until the next day.'

Fun for the balloonatics came to a quick end once they arrived at the front. Flight Sergeant William Lewis and Lieutenant Higman of the Third Balloon Squadron took off over Vimy Ridge in early May 1916. The morning started well. 'We were…enraptured with the glorious sunrise,' wrote Lewis. The euphoria did not last. 'Bang! Like a big drum being struck. Swish-rip-a sighing whistle, a noise, or rather a shriek like the tearing of some gigantic piece of canvas. Christ! What's happened? Gee. The balloon has burst. It has collapsed about us…'

The self-opening valve that released gas as the balloon ascended had not been properly adjusted; pressure from expanding gas had burst the envelope. Billows of balloon fabric buried the observers in their basket. They fought their way up for air. But the balloon was coming down fast; they could not wait around.

'We must jump', [Higman] said. I agreed with him and immediately dived over headfirst, and nearly dived through my harness. It had no shoulder straps, only a waistband and loops for one's legs. Never shall I forget that sickening horrible sensation when in my first rush through the air, I felt my leg loops at the knees and my waistband round my buttocks.' Then his parachute lines wrapped round the cable from the ground to the balloon. 'Suspended in mid-air! …I looked down and saw Lieutenant [Higman], his parachute getting smaller and smaller'.

The parachute lines began to uncoil. Lewis spun round and round and then was suddenly released. Now he was falling fast, with no resistance from the parachute. What happened next was not what he was expecting.

'Crash! I had shut my eyes, I thought I had struck the ground. No; in a slanting rushing dive, I had struck poor old H[igman]'s parachute, and the force of my fall had caused his parachute to collapse.'

'Sorry,' bellowed Lewis as they tumbled downwards, 'but I couldn't help it.' 'It's all right, old man,' shouted Higman back,' but couldn't you find some other bloody patch to fall on? Millions of bloody acres about you, yet you must pick me to fall on.'

'It looks like the finish' said Higman. It was not. Suddenly and unexpectedly, the Spencer parachute, with Lewis on top and Higman dangling below, billowed out. Their fall slowed dramatically. Lewis was thrown off the parachute, but managed to hang on to some of its cords. Shortly afterwards, Lewis landed, soon followed by Higman. Amazingly they both survived.

Better design of Lewis' parachute harness, which slipped off like a loose pair of trousers as he dived from the basket, would have avoided the near tragedy. The early Spencer parachutes were supplied without harnesses and units cobbled together their own. Nothing was done

fig. 66–67. Elsie Janis and Basil Hallam Radford. Courtesy of the Mary Evans Picture Library

about this until, as Alan Morris puts it, ' …a shock wave rippled along the British front and on to London, scores of thousands of soldiers having witnessed the death leap of 1 Kite Balloon section's OC, whose talents were recognised even in the Royal Circle.'

In the 1950s, you could still occasionally hear on the radio a song written by Arthur Wimperis in 1914. The first verse goes 'I'm Gilbert, the Filbert, the Knut with a K, the pride of Piccadilly, the blasé roué… I'm Gilbert the Filbert, the Colonel of the Knuts.' 'Knuts' were young men about town in the Bertie Wooster tradition. Basil Hallam [Radford] became internationally famous as 'Gilbert, the Filbert'. He and his 'sweetheart', the American Elsie Janis, were the best-known show business couple in England in 1915. Radford exchanged Gilbert's white tie, spats, monocle and tails for khaki and kite-balloon training in August 1915. He was sent to France a year later and became Captain in charge of a Kite Balloon section.

Soon after Radford's promotion, his balloon cable snapped while he and an observer were on a routine operation on 20th August 1916. The balloon shot up into the sky and off over the trenches towards No Mans Land. Radford insisted the junior officer jumped clear first and then jumped himself. As Radford left the balloon his parachute harness became detached and he plunged to the ground and was killed. This was a terrible public tragedy, rather as if Elvis Presley had been shot dead while serving with the US army in Germany.

General Trenchard, who became famous in the Second World War as a commander of air campaigns, called a conference of Kite Balloon Commanders. His Private Secretary, the efficient and wonderfully unsoldierly Maurice Baring, reported that the General pointed out that…'as the War continues…individualism…will have to give way to uniformity.' Trenchard had uniform standards for parachute harness on his mind. The meeting discussed

fig. 68. Observers in a balloon above HMS Emperor of India. Courtesy Imperial War Museum © IWM

Spencer parachutes.

'…MacNeece declared that Spencer parachutes were 'fine' but the fittings were bad.' Someone said that the parachute container caps were too loose and observers were afraid of the parachute coming out and yanking them with it. Trenchard agreed to order stronger containers and told his officers that he hoped that the use of a 'Calthrop spring hook' would mean that observers would not need to be tethered all the time.

Throughout the war Spencers had a competitor in parachute design, R. Everard Calthrop, an engineer who originally specialised in railway development. He worked on light railways in India and then returned home to construct and manage the Leek and Manifold narrow gauge line in the Peak District, one of the most beautifully sited railways in Britain.

Calthrop became committed to developing parachutes for life-saving from aircraft when his friend Charles Rolls was killed in a crash at Bournemouth in 1910. Calthrop designed his *Guardian Angel* parachute two months after the beginning of the war.

The RNAS had tested and rejected the Calthrop parachute for kite balloon use earlier in 1915, but its inventor did not give up and went through Rolls' mother, Lady Llangattock, to the sister of the First Lord of the Admiralty. An official wrote rather desperately to Maitland on the 20th December 1915 , 'What reply can I send to Mr Balfour's sister who is asking what the Admiralty think of this parachute?'

Maitland was not that interested, because he considered Spencer parachutes adequate for escape from his lighter-than-air craft. The Calthrop was also rather expensive. The Admiralty prodded Maitland for the trial results. 'The wretched inventor has done a lot at Chingford and has not yet had a reply.' Maitland finally responded on the 11th June 1916, 'I don't think myself the arrangement is required for standard machines.' Airships and observation balloons continued to be equipped with Spencer parachutes.

Calthrop's central demand was for parachutes to be adopted for escape from aeroplanes. *Flight* took up the cause in August 1917 arguing for general adoption of this 'useful accessory' and praising the quality of Calthrop's parachutes.

'General Longcroft, commander of the 3rd Brigade RFC in France, wrote as a pilot: 'I and my pilots keenly desire parachutes…' All was to no avail, however, the official reply being: 'This will impose a dangerous strain on the pilot.' (Lee 1968).

Robert Saundby , a World War 1 fighter pilot, wrote: '…it seems the military authorities took the view that pilots and observers might be tempted to abandon their aircraft unnecessarily. It was still believed that the gun, weapon or machine was more important than the man- a view that is very rightly no longer held.'

By the end of the war, many German pilots flew with a parachute tucked under their seat. Even the British War Cabinet knew by August 1918 that the Germans were jumping from burning planes. The French pilots had parachutes. But British pilots were still not allowed them.

John Lucas says with justifiable anger, 'Just how many pilots were sacrificed on the altar of official lethargy [is not known], but at least 250 are known to have hurled themselves from their burning planes in last desperate attempts to choose the quicker death…

Finally, on 16 September 1918, a declaration from the HQ of the RAF in the field gave authorisation that all single-seaters are to be fitted with parachutes forthwith. One feels ashamed to ask why it took so long.'

British balloon and airship crews took up Spencer parachutes to the end of the war. Dr Sansom, who had been a kite balloon observer, wrote to John Lucas, ' I had great trust in the Spencer parachute, though I felt nervous before my practice drop… We had no harness supplied at first, so I made a double bowline rope sling, which I always used, though our riggers made nice webbing slings for the other observers.'

Confirmation of the quality of Spencer parachutes came from Air Commodore Maitland (as he became) who in a 1921 lecture recalled that 750 kite balloon observers jumped using Spencer parachutes from burning balloons and that only three of them failed to open.

A family member might have monitored the qualities of Spencer kite balloons. Temporary Sub-Lieutenant Charles William Spencer, RNAS, the youngest of Percival's children, spent some of his war being towed above the Atlantic by Royal Navy vessels. He was in the basket of a kite balloon spotting for submarines, was often freezing and was, at all times, required to wear a collar and tie.

John Bacon, back in 1902, had been one of the first people to note (from a Spencer balloon) the possibilities of underwater surveillance from the air. By 1917, twenty two British ships were equipped to tow kite balloons. The balloons were particularly useful as observation platforms working with convoy escorts.

When Charles Spencer joined up in 1916, he was nearly twenty. He had worked for two and half years in a structural engineering office. But the officer who interviewed him at his Admiralty Pilot Test was interested in what Charles had learned in the factories just behind his house. 'Considerable experience in design and construction of balloons, kite balloons etc, also general knowledge of practical ballooning.' He had little to learn at Roehampton and quickly became a trainer. 'Since joining RNAS [he has been involved in] instruction of men in practical and theoretical ballooning.'

Charles worked at Roehampton for a year and then spent his war based at Shotley in Norfolk, and in the oversight of airship maintenance at Dunkerque in Belgium. By 1918 he was a Captain in the newly created Royal Air Force.

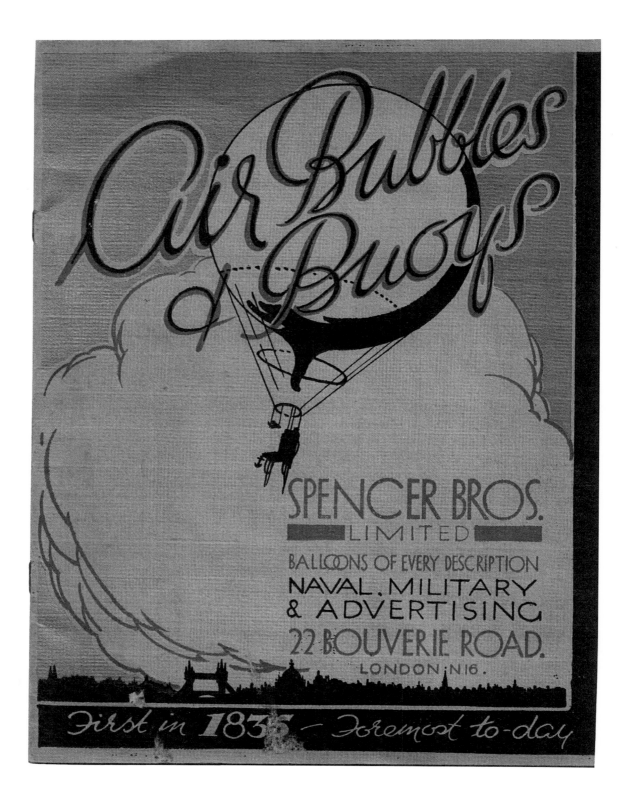

fig. 69. A Spencer Brothers poster from the 1920s

The end of the story

On the 9th February 1918 no less than 150 staff attended a party in Spencers' Large Balloon Hall in Highbury Grove, Islington. The War Office had bought great numbers of balloons, parachutes and other equipment for four years and the firm had grown spectacularly.

The war ended on the 11th November. A few days later, Lilian Tassena Spencer, Arthur's wife, (known in the family as Tassie) opened a new balloon hall just round the corner from Highbury Grove. Tassie knew what to say: 'Everyone [is] hoping to find work for all those employed during the war.' But everyone knew that peace meant unemployment for many. Marie Townend told my sister that years of stagnation for the firm followed as Government contracts came to an end.

Arthur resigned his directorship, moved up to Highgate Hill and died soon after, on the 21st February 1922. He left Tassie £21,196, a considerable sum. Tassie moved out of London.

Henry Spencer took over. He and, later on, his son, Percival Frederick, and daughter (another) Ena, began giving balloon and parachute displays at the events being scheduled again all over the country.

Spencers had a new parachute, the 'Salvus'. It was used for the first public parachute descent from an aeroplane in Australia in December 1919 when Captain Wilson of the Australian Flying Corps leaped from a plane at 1500 feet (457 metres). Similar successes were recorded for the *Salvus* in Air Ministry tests in the same year.

Everard Calthrop was still selling his *Guardian Angel* parachute which, like the *Salvus*, opened when the pilot's jump tugged a line attached to the aircraft. But the chance of Calthrop's, or any other 'fixed-line', parachute being adopted on either side of the Atlantic faded when Lieutenant Caldwell, RAF, was demonstrating the *Guardian Angel* in Dayton, Ohio. The plane's elevator equipment caught the line and cut it through. Caldwell fell to his death.

By 1921 international competitions involving lighter-than-air craft had come back to life. The Spencers entered the *Margaret* balloon in the tenth Gordon Bennett competition. Henry was the pilot and Ernest Allen, the firm's managing director, his co-pilot.

A fine snapshot of Captain Harry Spencer, the victim of the balloon tragedy (centre) with his son, Mr. Percival Spencer (left), and members of his crew. A part of the balloon is also shown.

fig. 70. Henry Spencer and his son, Percival, at the Rugby hospital fete, 9th September 1928

Fourteen crews took off from Solbosch gasworks near Brussels on 18th September 1921. The takeoff in front of 150,000 people was largely uneventful. But the ascent of the Belgian entry caused a sensation. Lieutenant DeMuyter and Alexander Veenstra soared into the air without realising that the ropes below their basket had caught up a member of their ground crew and were taking him up with them. '…women fainted when the unexpected passenger was seen swaying between earth and the clouds in danger either of losing his grip or crashing into the treetops skirting the field from which the gasbags left.' The crowd's cries eventually reached DeMuyter and Veenstra and they hauled the terrified man up into the basket.

The balloons left Solbosch in a south-easterly wind blowing them at 30-40 mph towards the Atlantic. It was reported that 'The Eiffel Tower wireless station sent out a request at noon to-day to all steamers in the eastern Atlantic, the English Channel, and the Bay of Biscay to keep a sharp outlook for the balloons… The Ministry of Marine also instructed all lighthouse keepers on the Atlantic seaboard from Dunkirk to the Spanish border, to be on the watch…'

Somehow all the crews survived, though a steamer had to pick up an American crew 15 miles off the Irish coast. The winner was the Swiss aeronaut, Paul Armbruster, who reached Lambay Island, off County Dublin, Ireland after flying 766 kilometres (475 miles) in 27 hours. He described his landing place: 'The island belongs to a British nobleman, Cecil Baring, but he had traveled to London with his wife the day before. His daughter, aged 17, welcomed us in the old castle from the fifteenth century in which no luxury was missing.'

Henry, Ernest and the *Margaret* were not far behind, though they missed out on the luxury. They travelled 667 kilometres to Strumble Head near Fishguard, in Wales, presumably about as far as Henry thought he could go without getting their feet wet. For his second place, Henry was awarded the Royal Aero Club bronze medal.

Spencers had a balloon in every Gordon Bennett competition for the next five years. In 1922, the *Margaret* took Henry and Ernest, now representing the Royal Aero Club, off from Geneva Gasworks and brought them 459 kilometres (285 miles) to Kuhbach in Bavaria and fourteenth place. In 1923, Captain Charles Spencer, RAF, now a civil engineer, piloted the *Margaret* up and away from Solbosch. He enjoyed ballooning and, like the Spencers who flew with Hedges Butler in the 1900s, had the wisdom to have a friend who was a well-off wine merchant. John Berry, of Berry Brothers and Rudd, financed the flight and became his co-pilot.

The flight does not sound much of a success. A passing ship rescued Spencer and Berry after they had ditched in the Skagerrak, the strait off the north west coast of Norway. But that is only part of the story. *Flight* described the 1923 Gordon Bennett competition as 'probably the most disastrous series of mishaps ever recorded against this ancient sport.'

During preparations for the launch, heavy rain was bouncing off the balloon envelopes. Four teams pulled out without even trying to take off. Then a thunderstorm reached the launch site. In the gusts, the *US Army S6*, collided with a Belgian balloon and ripped its net wide open. The American balloon exploded: it had probably been over-filled with gas and the collision was just too much for it.

Those pilots who took off could only climb slowly in the fierce winds. As they did so, they were blown towards nearby houses. They had to hurl out heavy bags of sand quickly to climb over the Brussels suburbs. Amazingly, no spectator was hit.

No-one called off the competition even then; balloons were leaving all the time. In their defence, the organisers could not have known that balloons were still flying through thunder and lighting after thirty minutes and more in the air. One balloon hit a power line and both crewmen were seriously injured. Then lighting struck three balloons and brought them down. Five of the six pilots died and the sixth was lucky to survive with two broken legs .

Most competitors only managed flights of between 50 and 300 kilometres; when they touched down in the Skagerrak, Spencer and Berry had travelled 1000 kilometres (621 miles). They struggled ashore and an elderly lady welcomed them to her cottage near the sea. She sat them down and prepared a hip bath in next door to wash off the weariness and salt water. John Berry went in first. Charles was soon startled by cries for help. 'What's going on?' he called back. 'She's trying to scrub my back.' A landing on water did not count, so the *Margaret* was awarded fourteenth place out of the fourteen balloons that had survived the competition.

This did not put Spencers off the Gordon Bennett. John Berry found more money. The *Margaret* took off from Solbosch again on the 15th June 1924. The organisers had realised that autumn ascents risked foul weather. From then on, take offs were scheduled in midsummer.

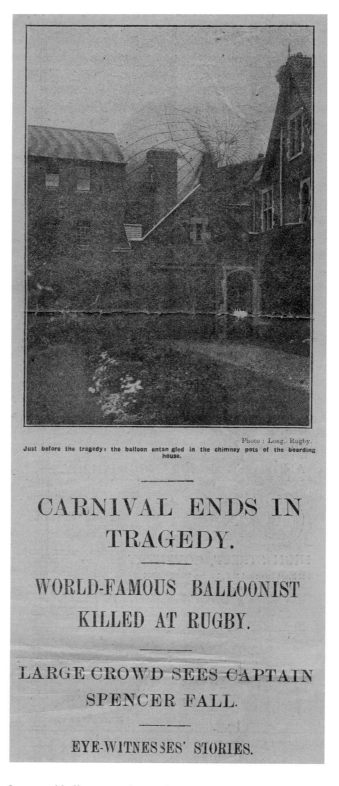

Just before the tragedy: the balloon entangled in the chimney pots of the boarding house.

CARNIVAL ENDS IN TRAGEDY.

WORLD-FAMOUS BALLOONIST KILLED AT RUGBY.

LARGE CROWD SEES CAPTAIN SPENCER FALL.

EYE-WITNESSES' STORIES.

fig. 71. The Spencers' balloon caught on chimneypots (Rugby Advertiser 10.9.1928)

The *Margaret* took a creditable seventh place: Charles brought the balloon down at Dieppe, 270 km (167 miles) from the start and convenient for the ferry that would take the pilots and the balloon back to England.

By this time the failure of the British Air Ministry to adopt a standard parachute for its aircrews was a scandal. The Americans had made the Irvin model compulsory for all their service fliers back in 1922. Finally Samuel Hoare, the Air Minister, announced the purchase of 2,261 Irvin parachutes for the RAF in March 1925. Spencers kept trying: Pathe filmed a Captain H. Spencer (almost certainly Henry) jumping over Stag Lane airfield in North London wearing a parachute designed by a Colonel Holt. *Flight* reported , 'Almost immediately, the main 17ft parachute was withdrawn from the pack and Captain Spencer continued the rest of his "fall" with a steady descent by its aid… In short, the demonstration was a success in every way.' But Irvins kept the British government parachute contracts.

1925 brought a commercial opportunity. The Royal Airship Works at Cardington had built a kite balloon designed to go to 30,000 feet. Trials showed it was highly unstable, so they turned to Spencers. This was a big project: Spencers' prototype needed 119,000 cubic feet of gas. The balloon was 200 foot long , weighed 2 tons and needed up to 100 attendants to walk it from its shed to the launch place in any sort of wind.

Spencers' monster was no more airworthy than Cardington's effort. In trials in September 1925 it went up to 1000 feet, then lurched into a dive. The gas was driven into the stern and the balloon took up an undignified nose down position and stayed there until winched back down. Another trial on the following day was no more successful. Spencers went off to think again.

They came back on the 7th October, with 'curtains' inside the envelope of the balloon to prevent too much movement of the gas. But the envelope was ripped when it was only 50 feet up and almost all the precious gas was lost. That was the end of that project, though the balloon was put forward again for Air Ministry inspection in April 1928.

The 1925 Gordon Bennett competition went ahead as usual. Charles Spencer and John Berry entered a new Spencer balloon, the *Miramar*. Yet again, an easterly wind governed the competitors' balloons after their take-off from Belgium. Charles was probably happy to land in Normandy to win ninth place but others went on over the sea.

The Spanish *Esperto* caught fire after flying too close to the funnel of a rescuing steamer and Ward T. Orman, the American pilot of *Goodyear III*, completed a bravura landing on the deck of the Dutch ship *Vaterland*, which was sailing conveniently near his route. He and his co-pilot travelled on to port on the *Vaterland*, but were disqualified: touchdowns on ships did not count.

The relative positions of Charles and Henry in the social structure of the day were very different. All the other brothers were out of the aviation picture. Arthur died soon after his retirement. Herbert and Sydney had gone their separate ways. Herbert was running his pub, and Sydney (the 'flying pharmacist' in the words of his local paper) was running a chemist's shop in Sutton, Lancashire.

Henry was, at weekends, a travelling showman parachutist. During the week he struggled with profit and loss in the face of declining interest in lighter-than-air craft. Even the aeroplane makers, like Shorts, had to build barges, motor boats and perambulators to survive.

Charles was now a reserve officer, an amateur pilot and a gentleman, increasingly involved in his profession as a civil engineer. Charles Spencer and John Berry flew the *Miramar* 169 kilometres from Antwerp into a creditable fifth place, their last Gordon Bennett flight.

All sorts of commercial activity had a difficult time in 1926: weakened firms like Spencers just needed a misjudgement or a piece of bad luck to bring them down. The first horror, surprisingly, involved the experienced airship designer E.T. (Tom) Willows. Henry Spencer booked him for the lowly role of 'pilot' of a captive balloon at Kempston Flower Show near Bedford on 3rd August 1926. His job was to take the balloon up to a hundred feet or so, allow the passengers a decent interval to admire the view and then chat to them as they were winched down to the ground.

The rides were popular. The balloon had made a dozen or so journeys with passengers paying two shillings each for the trip. On the final ascent, four passengers were in the basket of the *Miramar*, the same balloon used for the Gordon Bennett competitions. Willows was sitting above on a ring under the envelope. A police account says, 'The balloon was attached to a thick rope, which wound onto the roller of a motor winch on the ground… When descending, the rope became fouled in a tree…' Willows shouted 'For God's sake, pull us down!' to people below.

The balloon lifted the first group of men who grabbed the rope into the air. More joined them until a hundred or so were heaving at the rope and the balloon was coming down. All should have been well, but then, 'Suddenly a sharp crack was heard and the netting which held the basket to the balloon broke. This was quickly followed by the basket itself breaking away and falling 100 feet to the ground.'

Willows and one passenger were killed instantly. Two others died shortly afterwards and another was taken to Bedford General Hospital and died the following day. The passengers were all Kempston residents: the deaths were a local and national sensation. 2000 attended the funerals in Kempston Church.

C.G. Spencer and Sons Ltd was never going to escape unscathed, though the extent to which their staff were blameworthy was debated. The helpers who pulled at the rope may have put unusual pressures on the netting round the balloon envelope, but this would not necessarily have done such damage. The netting may have been in a poor state.

The real issue was probably Willows' decision to 'fly' the balloon in the first place. Such an experienced pilot must have known the risks. No-one can predict every gust of wind, but perhaps the Spencer team was desperate for the money and thought they could get in one last flight before conditions worsened.

Expert witnesses at the inquest stressed that it was an unusual accident. The jury brought in a verdict of accidental death. But the tragedy involved a distinguished aeronaut and innocent citizens on a 20 minute trip in a captive balloon. A prosecution followed :

'Arising out of the balloon accident at Kempston, Bedford, on August 3 last, when Captain ET Willows and four passengers were killed, proceedings, under the Air Navigation Consolidation order of 1923, and the Air Navigation Act of 1920, were taken against C.G.Spencer and Sons, Ltd, of Highbury, for allowing a balloon to be flown without special permission, and without it being certified as air-worthy. The magistrates convicted on both summonses. In the case of the failure to have a permit they imposed a fine of £100. With regard to the failure to have an air-worthiness certificate, they agreed that the phrasing of the temporary certificate was ambiguous, and imposed a penalty of £50.
Costs were fixed at 30 guineas.'

Besides the fines and costs, Henry gave a hundred guineas to the fund set up to support the bereaved families. Damage to the firm's reputation must have been more harmful than any financial loss.

Another terrible blow came in 1928. On the 9th September, Henry and his son Percival were at a hospital fete in Rugby. Percival went up in his balloon but was almost immediately forced down by a heavy rainstorm. The balloon became entangled with the chimney pots of a two storey building. Percival got down unscathed, but Henry, now aged 51, climbed up to recover the balloon. As he worked, he breathed in gas still in the balloon's envelope and was overcome. He fell 50 feet from the roof and was killed.

Young Percival then took over the firm. He managed to keep it going on a small scale until 1938, when he was suddenly taken ill and died at the very young age of 28. His sister, Ena, then took up the baton but soon, according to Marie Townend, sold the company to a Belgian.

The gymnastics side was still going. By 1901, George Spencer had been joined in the business by Cuvier ('Cuvie') and Edward his sons. In contrast to the balloon manufacturing side of the family, where technical ascendancy was lost by 1905, the firm stayed at the head of the game through the 1900s and beyond. Sales of wooden vaulting horses and parallel bars to the military and school boards provided the bread-and-butter income; but they won the glamorous contracts with equipment which used electrical and other technical developments.

By 1910 George was 76 and had pretty well retired; Messrs Heath and George, from a long established North London gymnastic equipment business, became directors. The most tragic and famous commission of the firm, now called Spencer, Heath and George, was the gymnasium of the *Titanic* built by Harland and Wolff in 1912. (Spencers furnished gymnasia for *Titanic* and her sister ship, the *Olympic*.) The gym had elegant arched windows, framed in teak looking out on the starboard boat deck. It was next to the first class accommodation, though second class passengers, men and women, could use its resources, and was immediately accessible from the spectacular grand staircase.

The gym was not big, but was crammed with equipment. You could row on the rowing machines, wallop the punch bag or pedal away on a stationary electric bicycle while admiring your progress on the huge dial in front of you. When that palled, you could work out on an electric horse or, wonder of wonders, take a gallop on the electric camel. An instructor, Thomas McCawley, always dressed smartly in white singlet and flannels, oversaw this feast of physical delights.

A *Titanic* survivor, Lawrence Beesley, a school master from Dulwich College, toured the ship before she sailed.

'Between the time of going on board and sailing, I inspected, in the company of two friends who had come from Exeter to see me off, the various decks, dining-saloons and libraries… We wandered casually into the gymnasium on the boatdeck…More passengers came in, and the instructor ran here and there, looking the very picture of robust, rosy-cheeked health and "fitness" in his white flannels, placing one passenger on the electric "horse," another on the "camel," while the laughing group of onlookers watched the inexperienced riders vigorously shaken up and down as he controlled the little motor which made the machines imitate so realistically horse and camel exercise.'

The gymnasium was part of a sports complex which included a Turkish bath, a squash court and a swimming pool. Ladies could use the gymnasium between 9 a.m. and noon, gentlemen from 2 p.m. and 6 p.m and children between 1 p.m. and 3 p.m. The Purser would sell you a shilling ticket for one session.

The story of the *Titanic* is part of popular culture. She sailed on Wednesday, April 10, 1911, with 2208 passengers and crew, on her maiden voyage to New York. She called at Cherbourg on the same day and went on to Queenstown in Ireland on the Thursday. That afternoon she left for New York. But on Sunday night at 11.45 P.M, the *Titanic* collided with an iceberg and sank within three hours.

According to Beesley, Thomas McCawley never left his post in the gym that night.

fig. 72. The gymnasium on the Titanic, March 1912, Robert John Welch

'It is related that on the night of the disaster, right up to the time of the Titanic's sinking, while the band grouped outside the gymnasium doors played with such supreme courage in face of the water which rose foot by foot before their eyes, the instructor was on duty inside, with passengers on the bicycles and the rowing-machines, still assisting and encouraging to the last. Along with the bandsmen it is fitting that his name, which I do not think has yet been put on record – it is McCawley – should have a place in the honourable list of those who did their duty faithfully to the ship and the line they served.'

John Jacob Astor and his pregnant teenage wife Madeline spent some of their last minutes together riding the horses in the gymnasium, where Astor tried to re-assure his wife about his chances of survival by cutting open a lifejacket and showing her the cork inside it. Then they both headed for a lifeboat: Second Officer Lightoller took Madeline on board but turned Astor away.

In 1985 Robert Ballard touched his submarine *Alvin* down on the deck just outside the Titanic's gymnasium. The team took some photographs through the gymnasium windows; the Spencer exercise equipment could still be seen. It will not be seen any more: in the last few years, the roof of the gymnasium has collapsed.

My father remembered his grandfather George Spencer as a kindly and rather handsome old man and Kate, his wife, as 'a dear and very sweet person who would not accept anything approaching a slight. She heard another visitor in a hotel refer to her as the 'old lady with a wig'. The hair was her own and she said so!'

fig. 73. George and Kate Spencer (sitting) with their daughter, Amy, and her husband, George Dickeson

George died in 1916 at the age of 93. He outlived every one of his brothers and sisters and several of his nephews and nieces as well. He left £7802 to Kate and his children.

Between the wars the firm remained popular with the builders of great liners. They fitted out the two gymnasia of the *Queen Mary* for Cunard in 1934. Some Spencer equipment can be seen at the ship's final resting place at Long Beach, California. Photographs of the first class gymnasium, which was gutted in the ship's conversion into a tourist attraction after 1968, suggest that it offered updated versions of much of what was available to the *Titanic* and *Olympic*'s passengers. The equipment included 'two horse riding machines, a double cycling machine, two hydraulic rowing machines, two belt vibrators [sic], two vibrating chairs'.

Queen Mary was the last word in Art Deco design and the gymnasium received its share of critical attention. The *Shipbuilder* magazine noted that the floor was laid 'with Korkoid [linoleum] in a striking design with large squares in black and white marble, and with borders in the same colours.' The walls were given a shaded effect 'secured by the use of seven different timbers disposed in horizontal bands'. A large frieze, one foot six inches in depth, went right round the room. 'This feature is decorated in humorous fashion by coloured caricatures of well-known international sporting characters ...executed by Mr Tom Webster.'

The business was still filing patents for bicycle pedals and balance beams in the early 1960s. By then there was no Spencer involvement and many directors' signatures had slipped in and out of the balance sheets. Its parent firm, the Olympic Gymnasium Company, finally wound up Spencer, Heath and George in 1978.

Afterthoughts

I first learned about the Spencers when I was very young. My grandmother, George Spencer's daughter, left us family papers that lived in a wooden chest in our hall. At some point it was established that I would write up or at least become the archivist for the records. But I was slow off the mark, and was grateful that my sister Gill and my father followed up contacts in the 1960s and 70s.

Spencer stories sometimes came to me. I was teaching in Woodberry Down School, Hackney, where a young cousin, Ruth Fryer, was a pupil. I went to meet Ruth and her mother, Marion, and we had a chat about the Spencers and their balloons. Marion told me that as a child her knickers were always made of parachute silk. Many years on, Ruth is a mother of three children, a PhD and a good friend.

Serendipity and some research has allowed the inclusion of new and unpublished material. I was lucky to find Alf Smith's records (discussed in Chapter 9) on sale at Sotheby's at a price I could afford and at a time I could manage in my lunch hour.

Then Alan Harvey, a cousin and genealogist living in Ontario, Canada, put me in touch with the direct descendants of Percival Spencer, who headed the aeronautical firm in the 1890s and 1900s. Graham and Dorothy Spencer and their children, Amanda and Charles, had unique material and generously gave me access to all of it. Sadly, Graham died weeks before this book was published. But he had read and approved virtually all the drafts in letter and spirit. He wrote about the title, 'Just right – it is the opposite of pompous.'

By March 2012 I had retired and could finish the book. 'Finish' is perhaps the wrong word. Digital publishing means that we need only print short runs, so, as long as anyone has the energy, we can update the stories as information appears.

Material comes online month after month: the Royal Aero Club's *FlightGlobal* site provides an invaluable reference point for all aviation since the 1900s; the Guildhall Library catalogue revealed the existence of a 1879 Puttick and Simpson auctioneers' catalogue of the sale of William Snoxell's fabulous automata. As email and text deprive the writers of family history of the handwritten letters they have had in the past, digitisation permits a wealth of other insights into people's lives.

Some of the Spencers' commercial practices were grubby, some of the rows, usually brother against brother, were over the top. Their businesses went up and down with the country's fortunes and priorities: emergencies, such as the 1858 invasion threat and the First World War, were sometimes the times of greatest activity. But Spencers also hunted down innovation, such as the German gymnastic equipment and the velocipede, and moved rapidly to exploit new, relatively inexpensive, ideas, as with their quick adoption of the parachute.

Percy Spencer probably understood the likelihood of the eventual dominance of the heavier-than-air machine. But with no capital and few connections to it, lack of social position and above all lack of the skills of the new motoring technologies, he could not do much about it when no government money was available. So Spencers' parachute teams kept on touring the agricultural shows and Bank Holiday fetes.

Demanding spectators sometimes pushed them into danger. Percy's risky flight in India was partly forced upon him by the threat of mob violence; in England, Marina Gaudron

Graham Spencer, with Charles Green's barometer, in 2012

(nee Spencer) was at Alexandra Palace on August Bank Holiday 1899 when her husband had to stay in his balloon to avoid the crowd's fury when his parachute failed. She told the *Daily Graphic*, 'The people will not be satisfied with proper balloon ascents; they must have sensations and people in our business must provide them. It is a pity the government do not put a stop to this sort of thing altogether.'

This sort of pressure could encourage accidents and financial stress made aeronauts even more likely to take risks. But Spencers generally managed their performances competently over the years while maintaining a safe standard in the equipment they manufactured. Between 1914 and 1918 their parachutes saved hundreds of lives and failed very rarely.

The parachutists often enjoyed something like rock star status and individual performers made good money during the summer. Dolly Shepherd received £2-10s for each jump, an improvement on the 7/6d a week she received as a waitress at the Alexandra Palace.

Dolly loved the ballooning and parachuting. Over and over again the early aeronauts write about the joy of flying. It is hard not to be caught up by the colossal optimism of chroniclers, like Harry Harper, for the spirit that the new technologies represented.

I would have liked to have written more about the women of the family and their exploits. Wherever I have found stories I have included them. But the men were always in the front line and the sources are hopelessly biased.

The ballooning business was an inevitable victim of the peace. By 1918 no-one had much use for lighter-than-air craft and fixed line parachutes. In contrast, the gymnastic equipment makers, Spencer, Heath and George, drew their jam from luxury liners, while schools and the military proved the bread and butter. It is no surprise that they survived to the 1960s.

I have enjoyed chasing down and recording the imagination, creativity and determination with which members of the family, men and women, pursued their interests for profit and pleasure. They have been great fun to be with during the years this book has worked its way to completion.

Chapters, people & dates

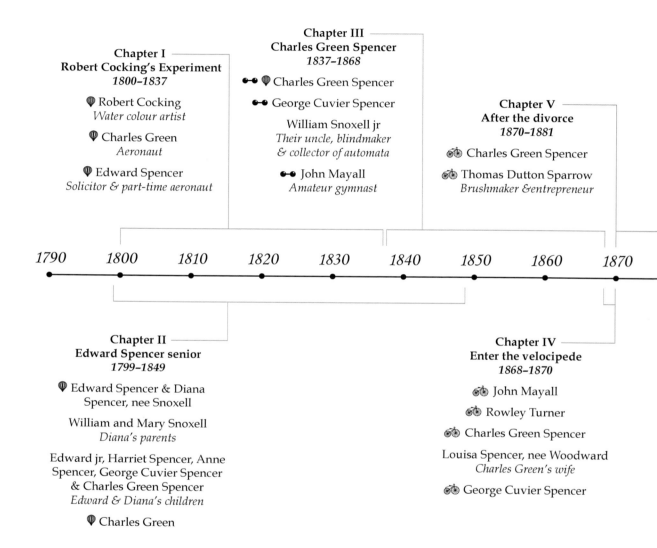

Chapter I
Robert Cocking's Experiment
1800–1837

- Robert Cocking
  Water colour artist
- Charles Green
  Aeronaut
- Edward Spencer
  Solicitor & part-time aeronaut

Chapter III
Charles Green Spencer
1837–1868

- Charles Green Spencer
- George Cuvier Spencer
- William Snoxell jr
  Their uncle, blindmaker & collector of automata
- John Mayall
  Amateur gymnast

Chapter V
After the divorce
1870–1881

- Charles Green Spencer
- Thomas Dutton Sparrow
  Brushmaker &entrepreneur

1790   1800   1810   1820   1830   1840   1850   1860   1870

Chapter II
Edward Spencer senior
1799–1849

- Edward Spencer & Diana
  Spencer, nee Snoxell
- William and Mary Snoxell
  Diana's parents
- Edward jr, Harriet Spencer, Anne
  Spencer, George Cuvier Spencer
  & Charles Green Spencer
  Edward & Diana's children
- Charles Green

Chapter IV
Enter the velocipede
1868–1870

- John Mayall
- Rowley Turner
- Charles Green Spencer
- Louisa Spencer, nee Woodward
  Charles Green's wife
- George Cuvier Spencer

Chapter VII
The best of times
1890–1901

⊕ Percy, Arthur,
Stanley, & Julia
Aeronauts

⊕ The Revd John Bacon
Aeronaut

⊕ Gertrude
*Bacon's daughter,
aeronaut*

⊕ Dr Berson
Scientist

Chapter IX
The great airship adventure
1902–1906

Mellins Food Limited
A baby food manufacturer

🐟 ⊕ Stanley Spencer
Aeronaut

🐟 Rose Spencer, nee Colman
Stanley's wife

Gladys
Stanley & Rose's daughter

⊕ Alfred & Ellen Smith,
nee Gardner
Aeronauts and licensees

Chapter XI
Spencers in the Great War
1914–1918

Arthur Spencer

⊕ Henry Spencer

⊕ Air Commodore Maitland
RNAS/RAF, aeronaut

Everard Calthrop
Parachute designer

⊕ Capt. Charles Spencer
RNAS/RAF, Percy's son

1880	1890	1900	1910	1920	1930	1940	1950	1960

Chapter VIII
Sister & brother aeronauts
1901–1902

⊕ Percy Spencer

⊕ Marina Gaudron,
nee Spencer
Percy's sister, aeronaut

⊕ Auguste Gaudron
Marina's husband, aeronaut

🐟 Alberto Santos-Dumont
*Rich & successful aeronaut
& pilot*

Chapter VI
CG Spencer & Sons Limited
1881–1890

⊕ Charles Green Spencer
Aeronaut

⊕ Percy, Arthur, Stanley, & Julia
Charles Green's children, aeronauts

Chapter X
Just airborne
1906–1914

⊕ Percy Spencer

⊕ Frank Hedges Butler,
the Hon Charles Rolls
& Griffith Brewer
*Members of the Aero
Club, aeronauts*

⊕ Henry Spencer
*Aeronaut, 4th son of Charles
Green Spencer & Louisa*

⊕ Auguste Gaudron

🐟 Dr Barton
Airship designer

✈ Herbert Spencer
*Aircraft designer & pilot,
youngest son of Charles Green
Spencer & Louisa*

Chapter XII
The end of the story
1918–1960

Arthur Spencer & his wife
Lilian Tassena Spencer

⊕ Henry Spencer

⊕ Percival, Frederick & Ena
Henry's children, aeronauts

Cuvier George Spencer &
his wife Kate, nee Coleman

⚬⚬ Cuvier George &
Edward Spencer
*Cuvier George & Kate's sons,
gymnastic equipment makers*

⚬⚬ Messrs Heath & George
Gymnastic equipment makers

Notes

Chapter 1

p.7 The early ballooonists often called themselves 'aeronauts'. The term appears throughout the sources and can conveniently refer to balloonists and parachutists

p.7 'he drew balloons because he loved them' *Stockwell News* 5.8.2011 www.stockwellnews.com

p.9 Gye and Hughes owned Vauxhall Gardens, funded the project and employed Green as pilot

p.9 The *Great Nassau* balloon (often known as the *Royal Nassau*) lifted 3797 lbs (1722 kg) at its trial: the basket and equipment weighed 997 lbs (452 kg). The envelope held 70,000 cubic feet of coal gas

p.9 ES: Edward Spencer wrote for *The Casket of Literature* so the identification is plausible

p.10 Gye and Hughes' concerns: John Bacon (1902) *Dominion of the Air* London: Cassell

p.12 Coxwell, H (1887) *My life and ballooning experiences* p. 72 . Henri Hegener (1964) What happened to Robert Cocking? *Flight International* 16.1.1964 suggested that Cocking and the parachute weighed 400 lbs (181 kg) in all

p.12 Charles Green refused to sanction any arrangement whereby he would be responsible for the release.

p.13 Cocking's injuries: see Hegener (1964). Dorothy Spencer Clarke writing in *Flight* a month later (27.2.94) confirms this account

p.13 In 1816 Faraday helped with Cocking's lectures for the City Philosophical Society at 53, Dorset St, Salisbury Square, near the home of Edward's parents-in-law. As Cocking was secretary of the society for ten years, Edward may have met him there. (Letter 68, *The Correspondence of Michael Faraday Volume 1* 1811-1831)

Chapter 2

p.17 Charles Dickens wrote to William Snoxell for an estimate for new blinds, 30.11.1839

p.21 The 'letter of friendship' is in the British Library collection *Aeronautica Illustra*

p.22 Christopher McGowan (2001) *The Dragon Seekers* Cambridge,Mass: Perseus Publishing has a good discussion of Buckland's career

p.22 Searles Wood's article: *Quarterly Journal of the Geological Society of London*, volume xxiii, page 394

p.22 The note can be found in the Royal Geological Society Library: Com P 2/181

p.22 Edward grafted the French naturalist into the family tree in July 1833 when he and Diana christened their third son George Cuvier Spencer

p.22 The specimen has now been provisionally reassigned to the related genus *Kentisuchus* rather than *Crocodylus:* C.A.Brochu (2007) Systematics and taxonomy of eocene tomistomine crocodylians from Britain and Northern Europe *Palaeontology* 50(4):917-928

p.25 'sufferings… to make one's hair stand on end': Lord Brougham, House of Lords Debate, 18.7.1844 Hansard vol 76 cc 999-1000

p.25 The tree resin copal was used as a varnish, for example for putting a shine on carriage exteriors. Mastic is a resin that you can use to chew or glue

p.25 Henry James described him as 'big, bearded, rattling, chattering, mimicking Albert Smith'. His one man show *Ascent of Mont Blanc* attracted 193,754 people over two seasons of performances at the Egyptian Hall in 1852-3. The opening night included 'four chamois and ten St Bernard dogs, two of which Smith gave to the Prince Consort and one to his friend Charles Dickens.' Richard D. Altick (1978) *The shows of London* Harvard University Press

p.26 'It is entirely typical': Rolt, LTC (1966) *The Aeronauts: a history of ballooning 1783-1903* Longmans

p.29 The note is in *Aeronautica Illustra* in the British Library. Gale, the other aeronaut mentioned, died a few years later on an ascent astride another unfortunate horse

p.29 The early months of 1849 were tough for the Snoxells and Spencers. Mary Ann Snoxell, William Snoxell's wife, died on the 24th January. The young architect S.J.Nicholl designed Edward's and the Snoxells' monuments in Highgate Cemetery. His most famous design is the 'Caradog Cup', now in the National Folk Museum of Wales

p.29 The £20 fee for a balloon flight: the Bank of England's inflation calculator suggests that £20 in 1850 would have bought £2280 in goods and services in 2012. www.bankofengland.co.uk/education/Pages/inflation/calculator/how.aspx. The site contains useful warnings about taking this sort of calculation as other than an approximation

p.29 Diana Snoxell, senior, mother of Diana Spencer, died in 1831, a few months after her husband

Chapter 3
p.37 Marina Woodward, nee Thomas, born in 1820, married James Woodward on 20th Feb 1835 (registered at Gloucester). The groom's full name is likely to have been James Brown Woodward, born in Bridport, Dorset

p.37 James is recorded as a 'licensed victualler' in the 1861 census. The couple, living with two daughters,were then managing the Dunstan Arms in East Road, Shoreditch

p.37 Westlake, R (1986) *The Territorial Battalions: A Pictorial History 1859-1985* London: Guild Publishing

p.38 The figure for volunteer recruits is in *Haydn's Dictionary of Dates* for 1906

p.38 'the ailments to which young girls are subject' *The Gymnast* 1.11.1890

p.39 Charles's skills: he won an award as the 'amateur champion gymnast' in 1863

p.39 'Charles Spencer [was] the first man to' Vivian,E.Charles (1920) *A History of Aeronautics*

Chapter 4
p.41 David V. Herlihy (2004) *Bicycle: the history* Yale University Press

p.44 Three Snoxell and Spencer velocipides have survived to the present day (personal communication from Nick Clayton)

p.45 'that have yet been offered to the public': other velocipedes were on offer at the time

p.45 Bob George's contribution: *The Boneshaker*, News and Views, February/March 1998

p.45 John Liffen's contribution: *The Boneshaker*, News and Views August/September 1998

p.45 *Brighton Examiner*, 23rd February 1869

p.46 The Hartlepool velocipede club: *South Durham Herald* page 9, 10th April 1869

p.47 The breakup of the partnership: *London Gazette*, 26 November 1869

p.47 Great Uncle George: George Cuvier Spencer

p.47 Grandma: Marina Woodward

p.47 Charles' bankruptcy: *London Gazette*, 24 January 1871

Chapter 5
p.49 The price of brushes: Beaujot, A (2012), *Victorian Fashion Accessories* London: Berg

p.49 www.british-history.ac.uk/report.aspx?compid=45909. Accessed 26.1.13

p.49 The National Museum of Scotland exhibit: a photograph can be seen on the nms.scran.ac.uk database:online reference 000-180-000-317-C. Accessed 26.1.13

p.51 The boomerang patent: *London Gazette*, 22nd March 1872

p.51 Sparrow's sponsorship of the John O'Groats ride: *Bicycling News*: 16.11.1877

p.51 Sparrow's work on tyres: Henry Pearson (1906) *Rubber Tires and All About Them*, p. 72

p.52 The Huna Inn: Hetty Munro writing in the *Caithness Field Club Bulletin* October 1982

p.52 Qui Vive's letter: *The Field*, 27th September 1873. Response from the Middlesex Bicycle Club's Secretary, E.Lucas,*The Field*, 4th October, 1873

p.52 Dissolution of the partnership:*London Gazette* 31st August 1875

p.53 'Vegetables… in moderation': some earlier health regimes banned all vegetables

p.53 In George's notice in the 1880 Post Office Directory: 'established 98 years'. This would mean the Snoxells' firm was founded in 1782. I have no evidence of this, though they may well have been in business by 1800

p.55 London's role: Gherardo Bonini London: the Cradle of Modern Weightlifting *The Sports Historian* 21(1) pp 56-76

Chapter 6
p.57 Percy was named after Spencer Percival, the only English Prime Minister to have been assassinated.

p.57 Percy told an inquest jury in 1901 that he had been ballooning for 29 years. This would give a date of 1872 for his first flight at the age of eight

p.57 Percy's education: *The Tatler* 138, 17.2.1904. Cowper Street College is now Central Foundation Boys School

p.57 The asbestos (Montgolfier) balloon is likely to have been a useful development: a spark had often turned hot air balloons into fire balloons

p.57 £35 in 1880 would have bought the equivalent of £3566 in goods and services in 2012; £150 in 1880 would have bought £15,281. Source: the Bank of England Inflation Calculator

p.59 The story of the argument between van Tassel and Baldwin, recounted by Dolly Shepherd, was current around the tea tables of the knowledgeable aeronauts at Alexandra Palace in the 1900s and carries considerable conviction. Other sources give the credit for developing the parachute to Baldwin.

p.59 Letter to Dorothy Abrahams,(later Dorothy Spencer-Clarke), Percy's daughter, from the Royal Aeronautical Society's Secretary, dated 28.12.1942, (now in the British Balloon Museum and Library). The Aeronautical Society of Great Britain was formed in 1866

p.61 Percy's triumphant return: Bacon (1902)

p.61 The scarf pin story: *The Tatler*, 17.2.1904

p.61 The Ramchunder story: Ghosh,A(1992) *Indian Journal of the History of Science*, 27(3) 1992

p.62 The monument of Charles Green Spencer and his family (originally the the Woodward family grave) was restored in 2012 by the Highgate Cemetery Trust with support from the Heritage Lottery Fund

p.63 The Dutch eventually crushed the Achinese in 1904

Chapter 7

p.65 British warship crews were cheap sources of labour on these tours

p.67 Gertrude Bacon became a distinguished aeronaut. The extracts are from her book about her father, *The Record of an Aeronaut*, published in 1907

p.71 Percy's advice to Andree: *People's Friend* (Dundee) February 1904

Chapter 8

p.75 The balloon factory trades: *Manchester Evening Chronicle* 15.2.1904

p.75 *Living London* celebrated London and its inhabitants' activities. John Bacon wrote the Chapter on 'Ballooning London'. George Sims (editor) (1901) *Living London* London: Cassell

p.76 The workshop held twenty or so balloons at any one time. *New York Herald* (Paris edition) 3.1.1904

p.77 His father told Graham Spencer the story of the daughters sitting on Percy's stomach

p.77 Viola Kavanagh was also known as Elsa Spencer, Viola Fleet, Viola Spencer-Kavanagh and Viola Spencer. Her real name was Edith Maud Cook. She was the first Englishwoman to fly an aeroplane, but was killed in July 1910 parachuting for the Gaudron team before she could gain her licence

p.77 Louisa Maud Brooks's death: Gaudron was probably running his own business by 1896. Press coverage of the story does not mention the Spencer Brothers. *South Wales Echo*, 23.1.2009; Nick Davey (2009) *Cathays Cemetery on its 150th Anniversary* Friends of Cathays Cemetery

p.77 Early balloon-making by the Short Brothers: Michael Donne (1987) *Pioneers of the Skies* Nicholson & Bass for Short Brothers PLC

p.79 Percy flew Conan Doyle from Crystal Palace to Sevenoaks on 4th July 1901

p.79 'Dirty Rolls': www.bbc.co.uk/blogs/wales/posts/charles-stewart-rolls-aviation-pioneer: accessed 25.5.13

p.79 Harry Harper (1956) *My fifty years in flying* Associated Newspapers

p.79 Ena was the family's name for Victorine Gaudron

p.80 C.C.Turner (1912) *The Romance of Aeronautics*

p.80 Major Squier wrote in *Flight* 22.5.09

p.80 The Zeppelin was 420 feet (128 metres) long and had fifteen gas-filled 'ballonets' inside the main framework: Robert Saundby (1971) *Early Aviation: Man Conquers the Air* Macdonald/ American Heritage

p.80 Alberto Santos-Dumont(1904) *Dans l'air* Paris: Charpentier & Fasquelle

p.81 'He had style...': Harry Harper (1956) describing Santos-Dumont

p.81 John Bacon (1902) describes the Buchanan airship

p.83 The police records of damage to Santos-Dumont's airship: MEPOL 2/598 101769 27.5.1902

p.83 The destruction of Santos-Dumont's airship: Bacon(1902)

Chapter 9

p.86 Patriotism may have trumped common sense on the choice of engine: French engines were considered far the best at the time

p.86 Marie was Mary and Percy Spencer's daughter, (Marie Townend in later life)

p.86 Ellen Smith's first jump: *Lancaster Observer* 23.5.1902

p.87 Rolt, 1966

p.88 The Gipsy Hill police warning: MEPOL 2/598 101769 14.9.1903

p.90 Preparing 30,000 cubic feet of hydrogen took 6,000 lbs of sulphuric acid, three tons of iron turnings [filings] and 10,000 gallons of water. It took five men ten hours constant work and cost £150 a time. Hydrogen gave 80lb lift per thousand cubic feet, coal gas only 35lb per thousand. *Liverpool Echo* 1.2.1904

p.92 The Gardner grave: http://www.users.waitrose.com/~radavenport/cemeteries/gardner.html

p.93 Stanley and the Prince of Wales: *Daily Mail* 15.10.1905

p.93 Percy's public contradiction of his brother: *Pelican* 18.10.1905

Chapter 10

p.95 Pollock and Dale's crossing: *Star* 5.2.1906

p.95 The flight of Vivienne III: *Flight* 29.5.1909

p.97 John A. Pritchard & Norman Pritchard (1986) *Balloons and Ballooning* Shire Publications Ltd

p.97 Charles Rolls and the Spencers: Driver, Hugh (1997) *The Birth of Military Aviation 1903-14: (Royal Historical Society Studies in History New Series)* Woodbridge: The Boydell Press for the Royal Historical Society

p.97 The Shrewsbury Show: *Shrewsbury Chronicle* 25/5/1905. £3043 in 1905 would have bought £313,331 worth of goods and services in 2012. The one shilling entry fee and the sixpence entry fee would have purchasing power equivalent to £1 and 50p respectively in 2012. (Bank of England Inflation Calculator)

p.98 If aristocratic titles weighed anything, many crews in the Aero Club's Hare and Hounds on the 24th June 1908 would have needed extra gas from the Club's main to get off the ground.

p.98 Colonel Capper's report is in the National Archives: AIR 1/728/176/3/20

p.99 Mrs Griffith Brewer on ballooning and the 'fair sex': *Daily News* 22/2/1906

p.100 Details of the booking are in the Shaw papers, Harry Ransom Humanities Research Center, University of Texas

p.100 Michael Holroyd quotes Loraine in *Bernard Shaw: the Pursuit of Power 1898-1918*

p.101 *Flight* notes that twenty motor manufacturers were showing aeroplanes at the 1910 Olympia Aero Show: everyone wanted a piece of the market

p.102 The Gnome: a popular French rotary engine

p.103 RF McFie, who gave his name to the *Empress* was famous at Brooklands for loathing scrambled eggs, which his landlady gave him every day. Michael Bradley & Percy Burn (1933) *Wheels take wings* Foulis and Company

p.103 Maurice and Henri Farman were talented French aircraft designers

p.103 Charles Cyril Turner (1927) *The Old Flying Days* The Arno Press

Chapter 11

p.105 Two other aeronauts, Auguste Gaudron and Henry Spencer, are also buried in Charles Green Spencer's family grave in Highgate Cemetery

p105 For example, Henry was staying with Gaudron and his family on the day of the 1901 census.

p.105 The RNAS separated from the Royal Flying Corps in July 1914

p.106 Usborne's letter is in the National Archives AIR 1/148/15/84

p.106 Alan Morris (1970) *The Balloonatics* Jarrold

p.107 'the German kite balloon caused considerable amusement among the Allies' troops on account of its shape.' (*Flight* 20.11.14). Presumably the soldiers laughed less when they realized the observers were directing accurate artillery fire into their positions.

p.107 *The Aerostat* magazine is the journal of the British Balloon and Airship Club

p.107 Edward Grosvenor's views:William Claxton (1920) *The Mastery of the Air 3rd Edition* London: Blackie

p.107 A woman parachutist, Kathe Paulus, invented the Paulus and her firm sold the model

p.108 The story of Lewis and Higman: C. B. Purdom ed. (1930) *Everyman at War* J.M.Dent

p.109 Gilbert the Filbert' was popular in the British army. The composer William Denis Browne wrote to another musician in December 1914, 'Think of me, fed on Tipperary and Gilbert the Filbert until they are bitten into my feet and into my brain.' *King's College, Cambridge, Archive/ PP/EJD/ 4/61*

p.109 Elsie Janis devoted the rest of the war to entertaining the American forces in Europe. An American officer wrote 'The British give their men rum before a battle, the French cognac, and we give ours Janis.' *New York Archives* Winter 2005 www.archives.nysed.gov accessed 26.5.13

p.109 Baring received the Legion d'Honneur in 1917. A heavy-handed French Colonel made the award: '...as I noticed he was digging the pins [of the fastening] deeper and deeper into my breast I finally uttered a shrill squeak. 'Maurice Baring (1920) *Flying Corps Headquarters* 1914-1918 Buchan and Enright

p.110 Major Foster MacNeece became an Air Vice Marshal

p.110 Correspondence on the *Guardian Angel* is in National Archives AIR 1/148/15/84

p.110 *Flight* (16.8.1917 p.837) encouraged the adoption of Calthrop parachutes in aeroplanes and noted a jump by a German airman from his crashing plane on 30.8.1917 (p.881)

p.111 War Cabinet and Imperial War cabinet minutes 20th August 1918

p.111 AG Lee(1968) *No parachute!* London: Jarrolds Publishers

p.111 Robert Saundby(1971) *Early aviation* Macdonald

p.111 John Lucas (1997) *The Silken Canopy:A History of the Parachute* Airlife Publishing Ltd

p.111 Kite balloon ship tactics: John J. Abbatiello (2006) *Anti-submarine warfare in World War 1: British Naval Aviation and the Defeat of the U-Boats* Routledge

p.111 Charles Spencer's records: National Archives 76-477-0-509

Chapter 12

p.113 The opening of the Balloon Hall: *Flight* 9.2.1918

p.113 The firm's fortunes can be tracked through the brothers' legacies: Percival left £4074 in 1913, Arthur £21,196 in 1922, Henry £1409 in 1928

p.113 *Flight,* 12.2.1920, reported on the Air Ministry tests

p.115 The 1921 Gordon Bennett competition: Associated Press, Paris, 19.9.1921

p.115 The 1923 Gordon Bennett competition: *Flight* 27.9.1923

p.117 The Stag Lane parachute demonstration: www.britishpathe.com/video/a-test-of-faith; *Flight,* 26.11.1925

p.117 Information on the high altitude kite balloon comes from the Barrage Balloon Reunion Society website: www.bbrc.org. The website says of the 1928 inspection, 'The Air Ministry was of the opinion that Spencers' did not have the technical ability and qualifications to produce a working High Altitude Kite Balloon'

p.117 Short Brothers after World War 1: Michael Donne (1987) *Pioneers of the Skies* Nicholson & Bass for Short Brothers PLC

p.118 Tom Willows made the first cross-channel airship flight from England to France in 1910.

p.118 *Flight* 11.11.1926 reported the prosecution after the Kempston deaths

p.119 *The Shipbuilder* souvenir issue 'Titanic and Olympic', from the Maritime Archives and Library collection. Reference number DX/1412

p.119 The sale catalogue of equipment from the *Olympic* in 1935 revealed that the horses were driven by a one horsepower motor; the camel only required a quarter of a horsepower.

p.121 The first class gymnasium on the *Queen Mary* was 36ft by 20ft and 11ft high. It took up a space on the Sun Deck between the squash court and the cinema. Original equipment can be seen in the museum of the *Queen Mary* at Long Beach, California. www.sterling.rmplc.co.uk. Accessed 22.6.13

p.121 Mr Chamberlain, who was manager at the Spencer, Heath and George in the 1960s, told me that all the Cunarders had mechanical horses and that they trotted and cantered realistically.

p.121 Tom Webster was a popular cartoonist who specialised in sporting caricatures. The British Cartoon Archive at the University of Kent holds a collection of his drawings www.cartoons.ac.uk/artists/tomwebster/biography. Accessed 19.6.13

Index of names

Members of the family and others who occur frequently in the book can be found in
Chapters, people & dates